ELECTRIC LIGHT ORCHESTRA

ELECTRIC LIGHT ORCHESTRA

SONG BY SONG

JOHN VAN DER KISTE

FONTHILL

Fonthill Media Language Policy

Fonthill Media publishes in the international English language market. One language edition is published worldwide. As there are minor differences in spelling and presentation, especially with regard to American English and British English, a policy is necessary to define which form of English to use. The Fonthill Policy is to use the form of English native to the author. John Van der Kiste was born and educated in England; therefore British English has been adopted in this publication.

Fonthill Media Limited
Fonthill Media LLC
www.fonthillmedia.com
office@fonthillmedia.com

First published in the United Kingdom and the United States of America 2017

British Library Cataloguing in Publication Data:
A catalogue record for this book is available from the British Library

ISBN 978-1-78155-600-9

Typeset in 10pt on 13pt MinionPro
Printed and bound in England

CONTENTS

Introduction
Biographical Overview

By 1966, many British and American groups who had started out and found success during the beat boom were increasingly dissatisfied with the limitations of guitars, drums, piano, and, occasionally, strings and brass. The Beatles and their producer George Martin threw down the gauntlet with the ambitious *Revolver*, The Rolling Stones with *Aftermath*, and The Beach Boys with *Pet Sounds*. Experimentation reached new heights a year later with albums such as The Beatles' *Sergeant Pepper's Lonely Hearts Club Band*, Pink Floyd's *The Piper at the Gates of Dawn*, and Procol Harum's epic single 'A Whiter Shade of Pale'—often regarded as the father of progressive rock.

Among the newer groups on whom this thirst for musical adventure was not lost was The Move. Formed in Birmingham around the end of 1965, their lead guitarist and songwriter Roy Wood numbered among his main influences Eddie Cochran, Tchaikovsky, The Shadows, and Bizet. Almost at once, he intended to break out of the beat group straitjacket. While they were recording their first album, he was thrilled by the strings, brass, and woodwind arrangements that their musical arranger Tony Visconti used on some tracks. He had started recording songs on his own, overdubbing all voices and instruments on what would become *Boulders*, his first solo album, but he also wanted to form a group using additional instruments like violin, cello, and French horn, playing more classically orientated music on stage. It would, he said, carry on from where The Beatles' 'I am the Walrus' had left off.

To realise this would involve expense that neither group, record company, nor management could afford. Yet Wood was aware there must be other young musicians playing cellos, violins, French horns, and other instruments, who would rather play in a rock band than an orchestra. He later said that hearing his songs performed with the benefit of Visconti's arrangements was when he began to become bored with The Move, 'because [he] thought there was something more to it than that'. The solution was for him and the others to develop the group's sound by adding more instruments and additional players, or else to plan a new group under a different name, using The Move to earn enough from hit singles and gigs to finance this brainchild until they could give it priority.

None of the others really shared his enthusiasm. When he drew them pictures of how his ideal group would look, including one with a cello section at the front and vocalist Carl

Wayne playing timpani, they refused to take him seriously at first. Drummer Bev Bevan showed some interest, but he thought it too risky to give up The Move—already proven as a consistent hit singles outfit—in pursuit of an ambitious venture that might not succeed.

However, at least one other musician and friend in Birmingham could see the potential of Wood's grand plan: Jeff Lynne—then vocalist, guitarist, and songwriter with The Idle Race. Lynne was convinced that success for them was just around the corner. By 1968, The Move were starting to unravel, driven in different directions by musical and personal differences. The two members who had initially created the group—bass guitarist Ace Kefford and Trevor Burton, originally guitarist and then bassist when Kefford left—had both gone by 1969, and Lynne was invited to join, but initially turned down the offer. At the beginning of 1970, once Wayne had also gone, Lynne was asked again and accepted this time on condition that The Move would temporarily continue, hopefully with more hit singles and as a successful live act, while they funnelled their creative energies into a new group. During one discussion, they considered using a large light show on stage like Pink Floyd. This focused Wood's mind on the BBC Light Orchestra—light, in this case, describing the style of music. If they were to use a light show and use electric instruments as well as electric lights, why not call themselves the Electric Light Orchestra?

In July 1970, just after The Move—now a four-piece featuring Wood, Lynne, Bevan, and bass guitarist Rick Price—had recorded their third album *Looking On*, they began work on '10538 Overture', a song developed from one of Lynne's ideas. It marked the birth of the first ELO album. After several months of sessions—during which Wood played bassoon, clarinet, and oboe, as well as guitars and cello; Lynne guitars and piano; Bevan drums; and guest musicians Bill Hunt on French horn and hunting horn and Steve Woolam on violin—it was released in December 1971. Favourable, sometimes enthusiastic reviews followed, not least one from *Melody Maker*'s Roy Hollingworth that it was 'the most relevant thing Harvest [the record label] [had] put out since the days of [Pink Floyd's] *Ummagumma*'.

Their long-delayed live debut took place in April 1972 at Croydon. This and their other initial gigs were generally erratic affairs. Several were poorly attended, with performers sometimes outnumbering the audience, classical instruments badly miked, and delays while Wood changed one instrument for another on stage. Compounding initial disenchantment and a fear that the public was not ready for them, even if the press was supportive, were growing differences between the two joint leaders. Wood and Lynne disagreed increasingly on musical direction, and Lynne was irritated that Wood, the better-known of the two, was getting nearly all the media attention and interviews. Such rivalry was fomented by management, which saw more money to be made from two groups than one, and after some ill-tempered exchanges in the recording studio, Wood decided to leave and form another group—Wizzard. From that moment onwards, Lynne was in full charge of ELO.

A complete rethink in the summer of 1972 led to the recruiting of further members, notably bass guitarist and backing vocalist Michael de Albuquerque, joining the nucleus of Lynne, Bevan, and classically trained bass guitarist-turned-keyboard player Richard Tandy. Audiences at live gigs might still have been small, but slots on BBC TV's *Top of the Pops* and subsequent Top 10 success for '10538 Overture', a modest chart placing for the debut album nine months after release, and a well-received show at the Reading Festival that August (sharing a bill with Wizzard among others) proved they were on their way.

Early in 1973, the second album, *ELO 2*, was released to mixed reviews and modest sales. It included a radical rearrangement of Chuck Berry's 'Roll Over Beethoven', which in edited form gave them a second Top 10 hit single as well as a more-or-less permanent encore on stage throughout their career. Moreover, after a carefully planned marketing campaign across the Atlantic, 'the little English guys with the big fiddles' became successful in America while they were still struggling to fill concert halls in a sometimes indifferent Britain. Ironically, 'Can't Get It Out of My Head' (their fifth single in Britain) was their first to miss the Top 50 at home, but it became their first American Top 10 hit.

Three years of new albums and touring worldwide brought their own reward. In the autumn of 1976, following the success of a Top 5 single, 'Livin' Thing', their sixth album (*A New World Record*) became their first to reach the British Top 10. It marked the start of almost permanent residency in the British and American charts. One year later, the double album *Out of the Blue* was hailed as an artistic triumph and remains their most critically respected venture as well as the parent of their best-loved single 'Mr Blue Sky'. In January 1979, they achieved the unprecedented feat of having a single album, a double album, a triple boxed-set album, an EP, and a single in the charts all at once. Fortuitously, the British record industry was unusually buoyant during the late 1970s, with several hit singles and albums selling in quantities only dreamed of earlier in the decade. Limited edition ELO coloured vinyls, 12", even occasional 10" singles, and picture discs helped to generate and sustain interest.

The eighth album *Discovery*, released that summer, gave them their first British No. 1 album, entering at pole position in the first week on sale, and being the first in Britain to generate four Top 10 singles—one a double A-side. In 1980, they topped the British singles chart at last with 'Xanadu', on which they had joint billing with Olivia Newton-John.

By then, the group had discarded violinist Mik Kaminski and cello players Hugh McDowell and Melvyn Gale, becoming a quartet comprising Lynne, Bevan, Tandy, and Kelly Groucutt on bass guitar and additional vocals, while retaining the services of Louis Clark, who had been their strings arranger for several years. Increasingly tired of touring, Lynne made no secret of preferring the creativity of the recording studio. With the advent of music videos, playing on stage night after night was now less essential to promote each successive release throughout Britain, America, and beyond. The group fragmented further in 1983 when Groucutt, who had played bass guitar on only three tracks on *Secret Messages*, sued Lynne and the group's management for unpaid royalties, and received a substantial settlement out of court. Bevan was increasingly marginalised by the ever more prevalent use of drum programming, and his part-time membership with Black Sabbath while they were on tour led to speculation that he had left his old group to join another.

By 1986, the group had become a trio as far as recording purposes went. *Balance of Power* was the album that completed Lynne's contractual obligations as leader of ELO. A few live dates that same year—one as co-headliners at a Birmingham charity concert and a few in Europe—saw them augmented by additional musicians, including the reappearance of violinist Mik Kaminski. Lynne then put ELO on indefinite hiatus to concentrate more on working with other artists.

In 1988, Bevan suggested they should reunite for another ELO album. When Lynne said no, Bevan and several members of the old group, some of whom—notably Groucutt and Kaminski—had formed the splinter group OrKestra, recruited additional musicians, and reformed as ELO Part II, a name settled on after protracted legal negotiations with Lynne. They recorded two albums of mostly self-penned material in the 1990s; the first was with Bevan and the three new members (keyboard player Eric Troyer, guitarist Pete Haycock, and Neil Lockwood) all sharing lead vocals, and the second was with Phil Bates replacing the latter two. Extensive worldwide tours were undertaken, including one with the Moscow Symphony Orchestra, featuring their own songs on stage alongside old favourites, but they never shook off the disappointment of a world that saw them as little more than a tribute band without the presence of their former leader. Some compared it to how The Beatles might have sounded after drafting in replacements for Lennon and McCartney, while one reference work said that ELO without Jeff Lynne was like a toaster without a plug.

In 1987, an invitation to Lynne to produce George Harrison's *Cloud Nine*, the former Beatle's most successful solo work for over a decade, led to both forming what became rock's ultimate supergroup a year later: The Traveling Wilburys, with Bob Dylan, Tom Petty, and Roy Orbison. The latter died a few weeks after the release of their first album, but the other four recorded a second two years later. Around 1989, Lynne collaborated with Roy Wood for the first time since their fractious sessions for the second album, to write and record two numbers together from start to finish, 'Me and You' and 'If You Can't Get What You Want'. Nearly thirty years later, these still await official release.

In 1990, Lynne released his first solo album, *Armchair Theatre*. As a producer, he achieved his highest profile when asked to take the place of George Martin, by then largely retired because of impaired hearing. In 1994, he worked with the three surviving Beatles to complete two 'new' tracks, 'Free as a Bird' and 'Real Love', based on demos recorded on cassette by John Lennon in the two or three years before his death. The results, issued on singles as well as on the *Anthology* CDs and television series soundtrack, made a graceful conclusion to the Fab Four's recording career.

In 1999, Bevan sold his rights to the ELO Part II name back to Lynne, who had just begun recording what would be the first album under the group name for fifteen years. Although largely a solo effort, *Zoom* featured guest musicians on some tracks, including Richard Tandy, George Harrison (making almost his last appearances on record prior to his death), Ringo Starr, and Rosie Vela. An American tour was scheduled but cancelled after disappointing ticket sales, and Lynne returned to producing other artists, including Joe Walsh and Regina Spektor.

After several years of rumours concerning the imminent emergence of new product, in 2012, he issued *Long Wave*, a second solo album featuring cover versions of old standards, as well as another ELO set, *Mr Blue Sky*, featuring rerecordings of their greatest hits alongside one new song. Their simultaneous release coincided with the screening of a television documentary, *Mr Blue Sky: The Story of Jeff Lynne and ELO*, as part of a themed Jeff Lynne night on 5 October 2012 on BBC4 with repeats of the *Rock Family Trees* documentary first shown in 1994, which traced the history of The Move, ELO, and associated Birmingham groups; of the June 1978 ELO Wembley concert; and of *Acoustic Live from Bungalow Palace*, featuring his solo performances of ELO songs accompanied by Tandy on piano. One week later, the albums entered the British chart at Nos 7 and 8 respectively, alongside a re-entry of the compilation *All Over the World*, a steady seller since its release in June 2005, at No. 10.

In November 2013, he played two songs at a Children in Need show with the BBC Concert Orchestra. His enthusiastic reception ultimately led to a full concert at Hyde Park in September 2014 accompanied by the orchestra and Take That's touring band, billed as Jeff Lynne's ELO. Overwhelmed by the general reaction from fans and unanimously glowing reviews throughout a media that had for some time been somewhat dismissive about the group, Lynne realised that the pendulum had swung back firmly in his favour. The result was his first fresh album for fourteen years, *Alone in the Universe*, recorded almost completely solo. Its reception and success encouraged him to undertake a full concert tour beginning in 2016, with dates selling out almost immediately, and including a performance at Glastonbury that summer. This renewed activity prompted a resurgence in sales of *All Over the World*, which not only re-entered the Top 10, but after eleven years in the shops, it finally reached No. 1. The music of ELO, which had seemed unfashionable for so long and then became a 'guilty pleasure', had returned to general favour once again. In April 2017, the group were inducted into the Rock and Roll Hall of Fame in New York.

This book examines every song on every ELO album, as well as those by ELO Part II. Several musicians have passed through the groups' ranks, either as full members on the albums or as part of the stage line-up. Some have released albums and singles as solo artists, as part of duos, and of larger ensembles. I have also included solo albums by those who were full members on record, namely Jeff Lynne, Roy Wood, Michael de Albuquerque, Kelly Groucutt, and as-close-as-they-get-without-having-their-picture-on-the-cover member Louis Clark (without the Royal Philharmonic Orchestra), while excluding collaborations such as The Tandy-Morgan Band, Violinski, The Move, Wizzard, and The Traveling Wilburys.

Three of ELO's albums, namely *On the Third Day*, *Eldorado*, and *Face the Music*, did not make the British charts on original release between 1973 and 1975. They were issued together in 1978 as a boxed set, *Three Light Years*, reaching No. 38 in Britain the following year.

All songs are written by Jeff Lynne unless indicated otherwise.

Michael de Albuquerque's name is sometimes given as Mike d'Albuquerque on ELO sleeve credits; I have used the fuller style, as on his solo albums.

For various reasons, original releases of several albums did not credit all musicians and vocalists—omissions that were addressed in the packaging of CD reissues. This book likewise aims to acknowledge all names involved where possible.

They say that to steal from one source is plagiarism, while to steal from several is research, and the same principle exists in rock music. As Keith Richards once said: 'There's only one song, and Adam and Eve wrote it; the rest is a variation on a theme'. Like The Beatles, Bob Dylan, and Led Zeppelin (and everybody else), ELO were heavily influenced by their favourites—to the extent that echoes of other peoples' songs can be heard in their own material. To suggest that '10538 Overture' or 'Mr Blue Sky' might sound like a well-known song by The Beatles or anyone else is not to accuse Jeff Lynne of infringing somebody else's copyrights so much as to acknowledge the obvious, and also to help give the reader a clearer idea of what it sounds like.

As for any meanings behind the songs, readers will find a mix of my own interpretations, such as they are, of Lynne's own thoughts from interviews and liner notes to CDs, and of the theories of others. In some cases, these are far better-informed than mine could ever be.

My thanks go to Martin Kinch for advice, information, and access to material from his collection; Rob Caiger, Gill at Magic Arts, Marc Haines, Andrew Whiteside, and Miles Tredinnick, for allowing their brains to be generously picked during writing and research, and help in various other ways; to Michael de Albuquerque, for information about his solo albums; to Jeff Cooper, for his excellent photographs; to all authors and webmasters of books and websites cited in the bibliography, especially Keith James Sinclair at ELO/Beatles Forever (elobeatlesforever.blogspot.co.uk) and Robert Porter at the Jeff Lynne Song Database (www.jefflynnesongs.com); to my wife, Kim, for her support as ever; and to Alan Sutton, Jay Slater, Steve Lambe, and Josh Greenland at Fonthill Media.

1

Electric Light Orchestra

The Electric Light Orchestra

UK:	Released December 1971, Harvest, No. 32
US:	Released March 1972, United Artists, No. 196, as *No Answer*
Current edition:	EMI CD
Personnel:	Roy Wood: vocals, cello, oboe, acoustic guitar, bass guitar, string bass, bassoon, clarinet, recorders, slide guitar, percussion Jeff Lynne: vocals, piano, electric guitar, bass guitar, percussion Bev Bevan: drums and percussion Bill Hunt: French horn, hunting horn Steve Woolam: violin

Recorded at Philips Studios, London, July 1970–June 1971
Produced by Roy Wood and Jeff Lynne

When the first album was recorded, ELO was a studio-bound project being launched by the three main members of The Move, who were simultaneously writing and recording what would be their fourth and last album, *Message from the Country*. A pretty bold step at the time, it sold steadily but not spectacularly, only entering the UK album chart after nine months. Following the Top 10 success of '10538 Overture' as a single, the album peaked at No. 32 during a four-week run. Fans who only knew ELO from their later days could be forgiven for wondering whether it really was the same outfit. Lynne was responsible for writing five of the nine tracks, Wood the other four, several showing something of a later Beatles influence. The record was summed up over forty years later by journalist Mark Beaumont, who said it 'let the classical dominate; pop hooks played second fiddle to lengthy baroque evocations of English civil war battles that couldn't have been more prog if they'd pulled on a fox's head 24 minutes in and announced supper'.[1]

In America, it was released in 1972 as *No Answer*, after a misunderstood telephone message from a record company executive at United Artists, who was checking up on the album name. Having failed to reach the ELO contact in question, the caller wrote down 'no answer' in the notes, and someone else thought that this was the album title. It has remained thus throughout over forty years of reissues.

A limited edition thirtieth anniversary enhanced CD in 2001, now deleted, contained two CDs. The first was a remaster of the original release, plus bonus session tracks, alternate versions of '10538 Overture', and a one-minute 'The Battle of Marston Moor'; there was also an enhanced section for computer, including memorabilia (such as press releases for the band and an acetate for the single), and a promotional video made for TV showing the group miming to '10538 Overture'. In the booklet accompanying the CD, Lynne called it 'a pretty wacky album, so innocent yet so bold'. Less charitably, in his 1980 book on the group, Bevan wrote that the album 'had been released to remarkably good reviews, despite being so awful'.[2]

Tracks

1. '10538 Overture'

The best-known, the first to be recorded, and arguably the finest track on the album opens with Lynne's electric guitar playing a short descending chord sequence accompanied by bass guitar, repeated with a French horn playing complementary notes, then joined by multi-tracked cello riffs and drums. It had initially been intended as a Move B-side, but as Lynne and Wood became more engrossed in multi-tracking instruments, it was seen as the obvious forthcoming debut ELO single. As soon as they started work, Lynne immediately thought they had something special with his big guitar riffs, while Wood experimented with phrases inspired partly by 'I am the Walrus' and partly by Hendrix on a Chinese cello bought for £30. In his words: 'We started overdubbing that onto this track we'd just done, and it started sounding like this orchestra we'd had in mind for all these months'. After bass and drums had been added, they listened to the playback, while Wood continued improvising on the cello. Lynne insisted that they add his further ideas to the track there and then, and Wood ended up playing at least ten cello parts. Bass guitarist Rick Price and drummer Bev Bevan had both had enough of the song for the moment and left the studio, allowing the other two to run riot in overdub paradise until, in their words, it sounded 'like some monster heavy metal orchestra'. Wood later erased Price's bass tracks and overdubbed his own.

As they wrote and recorded the vocals, needing a title, Lynne noticed the serial number on the modules of the recording console—1053. An extra digit was needed to make it scan, and it thus became 10538. They did a rough mix of the track and, *en route* to subsequent gigs (fulfilling their last few contracted bookings as The Move), they were demoted to the back seat, out of reach of the cassette player, in order to try and stop them putting the song on yet again. They circumvented this by bringing a portable tape player with two speakers, playing the song endlessly in the back 'to the point where it got up everybody's nose.'

The song's meaning has long been the subject of speculation. Lynne was often reluctant to discuss his songs in detail, but it is thought to be about an escaped prisoner on the run who has no name, only a number—perhaps in itself a comment on the depersonalisation of the individual in modern society. When pressed, he admitted to having written the lyrics about 'a nutcase' with a number on him, who was running about the place doing crazy things and ended up falling off a cliff, 'so it wasn't a happy song'.[3] Another theory suggests it is about a man who is trying to escape the system and ends up killing himself, hence the reference to a newsflash about somebody being found on the rocks by the bay and the question as to whether his life means more (after death, maybe) than it did before (while he was alive)—although there is no explicit reference to the fugitive being found dead.

The full album track lasts five and a half minutes. An edited version, fading shortly after the last verse and thus omitting about ninety seconds of the instrumental coda, was released as a single. Reaching No. 9, its success was a major factor in helping the album to enter the chart some nine months after release.

The song was covered by Bobby Sutcliff and Mitch Easter on the Jeff Lynne tribute album *Lynne Me Your Ears* in 2001, which featured various artists performing Lynne's compositions—mostly from the ELO catalogue, but also from those of The Idle Race, The Move, and The Traveling Wilburys, and also by Def Leppard on their cover versions album *Yeah* in 2006. Paul Weller's 'The Changingman', a Top 10 hit in 1995, sampled the main guitar riff. Lynne, who was not given a credit on the record, allegedly considered taking legal action against Weller. It might be noted that the descending guitar riff on '10538 Overture' bears some resemblance to The Beatles' 'Dear Prudence'.

When Roy Wood's Helicopters played several live dates between 1980 and 1982, the song was part of their set list, leading to speculation that Wood had written the song himself as well as co-producing and helping to arrange the original version. As for ELO, it remained in their set up to and including the era of 'Jeff Lynne's ELO'. In the mid-1970s, they would interpolate the opening chords from 'Do Ya' part of the way through, as heard in versions on their first live set *The Night the Light Went Out in Long Beach* (see p. 88), and in a concert at the New Victoria Theatre, London, in June 1976, released as 'Fusion' on video and DVD.

2. 'Look at Me Now' (Roy Wood)

This pastoral-sounding song unashamedly wears its 'Eleanor Rigby' inspiration on its sleeve. Lyrically, there is a feeling of mystery with its evocative, picturesque lyrics to somebody waiting and lurking in the trees, 'The King of the Castle [who] brought her to her knees', and a reference to 'the murder by the silver stream'. The backing is mostly multi-tracked cello, supplemented later with woodwind and horns, sounding like a medieval crumhorn, and a few seconds of acoustic guitar shortly before the end. It has similarities with Wood's 'Far Away over the Hill' from his first solo album *Boulders*, which was probably written and recorded earlier.

3. 'Nellie Takes Her Bow'

This story of a girl desperate to escape her unhappy home life and dreaming about a career on Broadway starts off quietly with mainly cello behind echo-soaked vocal. Without warning, it suddenly becomes almost a different piece altogether, with a brisk drum roll and some striking violin work—which sounds half-oriental, like a 1930s Palm Court ensemble—before horns and cello join in, playing riffs based on variations on a theme of 'God Rest Ye Merry Gentlemen'.

4. 'The Battle of Marston Moor (July 2nd, 1644)' (Roy Wood)

At six minutes, this is the longest track on the album. It also has the dubious distinction—if general opinion from fans' comments, particularly online, is considered a reliable barometer—of being the least-loved track in the entire ELO back catalogue. After a short musical introduction, a speech from Roy 'Oliver' Wood berates King Charles I for stooping to betray his own people and proclaims that he will raise an army so that every born man would fight to regain his own freedom. It then becomes an instrumental with mainly celli and drums, which Wood played as Bevan refused to because he disliked the number so much. Lynne probably had little input, and the track is presumed to be mostly if not completely Wood's own work. Multi-tracked recorders add a slightly Jethro Tull-like flavour, and it takes little imagination to visualise it as incidental music suitable for a Civil War film-related soundtrack. To dismiss it merely as eccentricity run riot or a tuneless noise, as some have done, does it less than justice. It may not be 'pop music as we know it', with an instantly hummable chorus, and is almost totally unlike anything else they ever recorded, yet one cannot but credit Wood for flying in the face of commercial expectations, experimenting eccentrically with styles from a bygone era, and adding something of his own at the same time.

5. 'First Movement (Jumping Biz)' (Roy Wood)

Wood admitted this second instrumental was inspired by 'Classical Gas', a Top 10 hit by Mason Williams from 1968, which he used to play in the dressing room before gigs; as such, he was inspired to write something similar: 'If you listen to it you'll notice that in fact they are two different tunes played in the same style'. Arguably the most instantly catchy tune on the album, it is a glorious mix of melody, acoustic guitar, drums, strings, and woodwind. The heavily overdubbed strings provide a fitting indication of the sound that would have its full flowering in Louis Clark's arrangements for the group at their commercial peak in the second half of the decade.

6. 'Mr Radio'

Lynne called this ode to the wireless 'a quirky one made to sound like a 1920s recording, deliberately having no bass part'. It starts appropriately with a few seconds of a radio being tuned in, followed by some backwards-sampled strings, then Lynne's piano, and an echoing John Lennon-like vocal lead into a song about a man whose wife has left him and that he now has only his audio for company. After the last verse, a passage on piano, violin, and cellos cross-fades with another backward sample. This and the music at the start of the track are taken from 'London Sketchbook', a collection of Mozart pieces performed by Sir Neville Marriner and the Academy of St Martin-in-the-Fields at Wembley Town Hall in August 1971, edited and played backwards. The first extract is from K. 15a-Ss-Devertimento in E Flat-2, K.15dd, and the last is from K. 15a-Ss-Divertimento in E Flat-3, K.15cc & 15ff.

Although perhaps lacking the commercial appeal of '10538 Overture', it was briefly considered as a second single. An edit without the first twenty-five seconds prior to the piano and start of the song, and the last thirty-five seconds of sampled strings, thus shortening it by around a minute, was prepared for the purpose. This was released on the compilation album *Harvest Showdown* in 2005, featuring fourteen tracks by ELO, The Move, Wizzard, and Roy Wood.

7. 'Manhattan Rumble (49th Street Massacre)'

The third instrumental starts sounding like a martial piece of film music, mostly piano with cello and drums providing a stately rhythm and woodwinds and horns producing a brass effect. As the tempo changes, the piano seems to be playing a tune from an old music box, after which more Broadway musical jazz age-style tunes take over. At around the three-minute mark, there is a brief vocal section sung in falsetto and accompanied by piano. It remained almost inaudible until a quadraphonic mix of the album was released in 2012, when careful listening revealed it was Wood singing the line 'Clap hands! 'Cos here comes Charley running up and down the city wall! Clap hands! 'Cos here comes Charley!' It was taken, with some modifications to the melody, from a 1925 jazz age song ('Clap Hands! Here Comes Charley!') written by Billy Rose, Ballard MacDonald, and Joseph Meyer, and later recorded by others, including Charlie Kunz and Ella Fitzgerald.

8. 'Queen of the Hours'

This was another dreamy number, with suitably enigmatic poetic lyrics. Who is the Queen of the Hours—a medieval European sovereign lady or a character from a Tennyson epic? Is the Isabella Creek in the last line the one in America or Australia or is it merely there because it scanned? Whatever, it is one of the prettiest songs here, with restrainedly crunchy sawing cellos and horns and a gentle acoustic guitar in one channel. Some have likened it to 'I am the Walrus' backwards, with others comparing it to a hybrid of George Harrison and Ray Davies.

9. 'Whisper in the Night' (Roy Wood)

This opens with a lightly picked acoustic guitar and church bell chime, which leads into a hymn-like song, reminiscent of the song that would later become Wood's first solo hit—the enchanting 'Dear Elaine'. Drums are notable by their absence. Choral vocals—(maybe Wood multi-tracked as on 'Songs of Praise' from *Boulders* or one of the school choirs he used on Wizzard's 'I Wish it Could be Christmas Everyday' or as a soloist on his, or Roy Wood's Helicopters, singles 'Sing Out the Old, Ring in the New' and 'Green Glass

Windows')—come in softly during the interlude, and it makes a peaceful conclusion to the record. Graham Bonnet, previously vocalist with Marbles and later with Rainbow and the Michael Schenker Group, released his version as a single the following year.

Bonus Tracks

10. 'The Battle of Marston Moor' (Roy Wood)

A one-minute fragment from an early session, this excludes Wood's speech and just comprises a brief run-through of part of the tune with cellos and woodwind.

11. '10538 Overture'

This outtake is about ten seconds longer than the version that was released and sounds very similar, with the exception of the end, which does not exactly fade out, but has the instruments gradually stopping more or less in thin air after attempting a live fade, plus a second or two of truncated studio chat.

First Light

Issued in 2001, this was the second CD that comprised the thirtieth anniversary limited edition reissue. It featured quad mixes of several tracks, plus three numbers recorded live for Granada TV's *Set of Six*, 9 May 1972.

1. 'Brian Matthew Introduces ELO/10538 Overture' (acetate version)

Matthew introduces 'a new sound with a new concept'. The recording is basically as per the album version apart from a very brief repetition of one phrase in the introduction.

2. 'Look at Me Now' (Quad mix) (Roy Wood)

3. 'Nellie Takes Her Bow' (Quad mix)

4. 'The Battle of Marston Moor (July 2nd, 1644)' (Quad mix) (Roy Wood)

All three above are musically the same as the stereo versions on the standard album.

5. 'Jeff's Boogie No. 2' (Live)

Introduced by Wood as 'part of a long line of Jeff's songs that he [could not] think of titles for', this is the number that appeared on the second album several months later as 'In Old

England Town'. Although understandably sounding less polished and more raw than the corresponding album version, it demonstrates that—in spite of often-repeated tales of chaotic, if not near-disastrous and often poorly attended gigs during the few weeks from April 1972 onwards—Wood was part of the line-up and they could deliver the goods on stage on such intricate and lengthy songs, which owed little to the conventions of less complicated three-minute tunes.

6. 'Whisper in the Night' (Live) (Roy Wood)

After a brief apology for having to sort himself out because his instruments had got tangled up in the electrical leads, Wood introduces this from the first album as a hymn that they recorded with a choir (in other words, presumably the multi-tracked lead vocalist himself): 'but we couldn't afford it tonight'. As well as the lack of choral embellishment, the live version differs from the studio one in that Wood plays electric, not acoustic guitar, and Bevan plays drums softly, although he was not in evidence on the original.

7. 'Great Balls of Fire' (Otis Blackwell and Jack Hammer)

An eccentric violin- and cello-driven variation on Jerry Lee Lewis's classic, this has the obligatory concession to rock-meets-classics in the shape of a few bars of decidedly quirky violin and cello between each vocal line at the start of the song. Further on are a couple more passages from the strings, which depart from the basic chord sequence. Lynne takes lead vocal and plays guitar, but does not opt for a more conventional lead guitar break anywhere, which he did when playing the song on stage a year or so later. Video footage of the group's performance shows Wood apparently, but more or less inaudibly playing saxophone. While the original version, a British No. 1 in 1958, lasted less than two minutes, ELO's rendition clocks in at five and a half, nearly three times as long, and finishes with a single bar from Beethoven's Fifth Symphony—soon to acquire a more significant presence in part of the ELO catalogue.

8. 'Mr Radio' (Take 9)

Fifteen seconds longer than the album version, this earlier take includes about forty seconds at the beginning and another thirty at the end of solo violin, instead of the radio tuning-in effects and the tape played backwards.

9. '10538 Overture' (Live BBC session)

Initially recorded for broadcast on Radio 1's *Sounds of the Seventies*, presented by Bob Harris in February 1972, this includes Brian Matthew's voiceover when the same recording was presented on the BBC World Service *Top of the Pops*, which had no connection with the BBC television show of the same name.

The Electric Light Orchestra: 40th Anniversary Edition, CD+DVD

Issued in 2012, this is the remastered original album, featuring the 1973 Quadraphonic mix in 4.1 surround sound, high resolution original stereo master, plus the original promotional film for '10538 Overture'. Disc 1 (audio) contains the nine original tracks, plus alternate takes, versions, and edits for five of these, including the proposed single edit for 'Mr Radio'. Disc 2 (DVD) features the Quad Mixes and the promo film. No songs that were not on the original album are included.

ELO 2

UK:	Released March 1973, Harvest, No. 35
US:	Released March 1973, United Artists, No. 53 (Cashbox), No. 62 (Billboard)
Current edition:	EMI CD
Personnel:	Jeff Lynne: vocals, piano, guitar, Moog, harmonium Bev Bevan: drums and percussion Richard Tandy: keyboards Colin Walker, Mike Edwards: cellos Michael de Albuquerque: bass guitar, vocals Wilf Gibson: violin Roy Wood: bass guitar, cello (tracks 1 and 4)

Recorded at Air Studios, London, May–October 1972
Produced by Jeff Lynne

In its original form, ELO's second album is unique among their back catalogue with having just five lengthy tracks, the two shortest being almost seven minutes long. More than any of the others, it placed them in the prog-rock category. It yielded one Top 10 single, albeit edited from its original seven-minute form to four and a half minutes, while the album spent just one week in the album chart at No. 35. Lynne was fully in control by this stage as Wood had left shortly after recording sessions began to form his new group Wizzard. He had played bass guitar and cello on two tracks, but was uncredited on the original release by mutual agreement. This was rectified in 2003 when it was remastered and reissued on CD with the addition of eight shorter bonus cuts.

Lynne suggested not long afterwards that it had been a mistake to record so many long numbers, something which he had thought obligatory at the time. He was not alone; the first Wizzard album, released around the same time, included one song lasting thirteen and a half minutes—considerably more in live performance.

In 2003, a limited edition thirtieth anniversary double CD was released. The first was a remaster of the original release plus eight bonus tracks, the second, *The Lost Planet*, comprised BBC sessions and various outtakes (see p. 26). In his notes for the accompanying booklet, he admitted he had tempered his views. It was 'a wacky collection' like the first, and he said that some of the songs were 'a bit longer than they might be' and that overall it was 'all very experimental and sometimes a bit over the top but [he felt that] it taught [him] a bit about where to go musically and where not to go'.

Tracks

1. 'In Old England Town (Boogie No. 2)'

A seven-minute epic that starts with interplay between cellos, violin, drums, and then lead guitar for almost two minutes before the vocals begin. It is hardly a conventional song, the lyrics being more or less blank verse integrated with musical passages of different time signatures. A close look at the lyrics suggests a satirical look at the political establishment, with references to the policeman's ball, where the boys in blue are 'all dancing in a line'; the military, where the soldiers are 'all marching round and round'; and environmental concerns—in old England town there was air where now there's smoke, so build more cars 'and drive away before we choke'. The instruments are for the most part sawing cellos and violin, underpinned by drums, guitar chords, and a few guitar fills, yet again recalling The Beatles. Lynne was still honing his craft of combining rock and classics, the latter being clearly heard in the way that, musically, each track is based on little musical movements, constantly varying in light and shade until a burst of electric guitar and vocal nudges it back into rock 'n' roll.

2. 'Momma'

A slow, mournful, even haunting seven-minute piece begins with a single note treated with heavy echo for about five seconds. After that, the violin and cellos predominate again, with tinkling piano and synthesiser cutting in at intervals. It finishes with a spacey piece about twenty seconds long on Moog. An edited four-minute version without the final section appeared on a 1991 compilation of Harvest material, *The Early Years*.

3. 'Roll Over Beethoven' (Chuck Berry)

The Chuck Berry classic that gave him a No. 6 British hit and a more modest Top 50 American entry in 1956 was one of only two cover versions ELO ever recorded on a studio album. According to Bev Bevan in his 1980 biography of the group, it was 'perhaps the most important single [they] ever made'. An edit of four minutes and thirty-five seconds was a No. 6 British hit (initially with 'Manhattan Rumble (49th Street Massacre)' on the B-side, then recalled and replaced with 'Queen of the Hours', both from the first album). In Britain, it peaked at No. 6, while it was their first American chart entry, reaching No. 42 (Billboard) and No. 48 (Cashbox).

The full seven-minute album version is a bombastic, splendidly over-the-top rearrangement beginning with a few bars of Beethoven's Fifth Symphony before Lynne cuts in with the Chuck Berry-style guitar intro and sings his heart out; while the cellos and violins battle away like crazy, Bevan punishes the drums and Tandy hits the ivories like a pub pianist on helium. One or two short passages with the strings help to transform what was a three-chord, twelve-bar rocker into a magnificent epic. It came at a time when ELO were trying to define themselves as a rock band with classical instruments as a key part of the band, including this and 'Great Balls of Fire' in the live set, this being an obvious choice because of the title and Tchaikovsky references in the lyric.

After Wood had left, it was adopted as their encore number on stage—up to the group's final gigs in 1986 and thereafter by Jeff Lynne's ELO from 2014 onwards—as a rousing number guaranteed to get any of the audience on their feet not standing already. The group initially prefaced it with a quote from Beethoven's Ninth Symphony as an introduction, then used the motif from the first movement of the Fifth Symphony instead, which was used several times on different instruments throughout the instrumental breaks in the song. Lynne deliberately used a cheap microphone so the vocals would have a rough, early rock 'n' roll feel, singing in a raw voice, and sometimes deliberately slurring the words as well for effect. He later commented that he thought the vocals did not turn out as well as he wished.

Although they had been performing the song on stage for a while, Lynne was unsure of the words and generally used to improvise them as they went along. After they had completed recording the backing track, they contacted Heavyhead Records, a record shop in Birmingham co-owned jointly by Bev Bevan, for assistance. Some sources say that somebody at the shop played the record and transcribed the lyrics for Lynne over the phone, but co-owner Ronny Smith claimed that he was on the other end of the phone at the time so he recited them from memory. Regardless of which story is correct, some lines still departed from the original, among them 'need a shot of rhythm and blues', which should have been 'the jukebox's blowin' a fuse', and 'go for cover and reel and rock it, roll it over' instead of 'a trifle further then reel and rock with one another'. Lynne may have been given the words of The Beatles' version from their second album *With The Beatles*, on which George Harrison likewise sang slight variations on the original. Lynne once had a chance to meet Berry, but chose not to as he was apprehensive of what he might have thought of the way they had treated his song, though their recording and performances must have boosted his royalties over the years.

The group recorded it in September 1972 in AIR Studios, owned at the time by Beatles' producer George Martin. He was in a neighbouring studio at the time, recording the orchestra on Paul McCartney's 'Live and Let Die'. When invited to come and listen to the work in progress, he nodded in approval and told them they had a hit on their hands. On its release as a single in January 1973, Radio 1's John Peel, at the time also resident reviewer for *Disc and Music Echo*, praised it as being 'corny, jokey and quite magnificent', saying that the strings, 'rocking like bitches, play sort of ghost-train evil', and that if it was not a No. 1 '[he would] come among [them] with a whip'.

In addition to the full seven-minute and shorter edited versions issued in Britain, the American pressing of the album featured a slightly extended version playing at eight minutes and eleven seconds, including an additional instrumental break—of the (superior) pub piano variety—shortly before the lead guitar break preceding the third verse. Its inclusion was apparently due to an error in the American United Artists office. Some European compilations also used the longer one. With the 2006 remastering of the album, it was corrected to the seven-minute version worldwide. The 1976 American compilation album *Olé ELO* also used the longer version by mistake, and within two or three years, it was repressed with the single version edit, although the timing was not corrected on the record cover or label. The seven-minute version appeared on *Flashback* in 2000, a triple retrospective CD compiled personally by Lynne.

In 1976, when talking about the recording of the album, Lynne stated: 'I thought you had to do long numbers, otherwise, people would think there was something wrong with us. So we had an eleven-minute [*sic.*] version of "Roll Over Beethoven", incredible. I find it impossible to listen to, now. Boring, really boring'.[4]

A few weeks after it was released as a single, Wizzard issued their second 45, the chart-topping 'See My Baby Jive'. The B-side was a jazz-rock instrumental, 'Bend Over Beethoven', with 'the official follow-up to "California Man!"' printed on the label underneath the title and composer credit. According to the label, it was written by cellist Hugh McDowell, who had left ELO in the summer of 1972 with Wood and Bill Hunt, although it is believed that Wood wrote the track and 'gave' it to McDowell as part of a policy of allowing fellow Wizzard members a turn at having a composing credit on the B-sides of singles to give them a share in sales royalties. However, it was taking the mickey, and as ELO were still smarting from the split the previous summer to the extent that it was a no-go area for music press interviewers, they were not amused. Nevertheless, there were no hard feelings against Hugh, who rejoined ELO later that year on the departure of Colin Walker.

4. 'From the Sun to the World (Boogie No. 1)'

This starts off with tinkling piano and synth, again, in melody as well as in mood reminiscent of Beethoven's 'Moonlight Sonata'. All things considered, the noted German composer provided more than a little inspiration for this album. During the eight minutes plus of this track, there is plenty of light and shade, with some vocals after the introduction and a gentle passage with violin and piano alternately taking the lead, plus French horn (uncredited, possibly Wood again), which seems about to bring it to a peaceful ending after about four minutes. Then it starts again with a brisk section led by classical meets boogie-woogie piano (imagine Jools Holland playing Rachmaninoff) before the vocals return, the strings join in, and a burst of super-swift lead guitar comes in (and is that a few seconds of siren we hear in the background, encouraging everyone to take cover?), before a frenzied coda led by strings and synth. Few of ELO's songs ever bore out Lynne's plans to combine rock 'n' roll and the classics more so than this one.

As for the subtitle, according to those in the inner group circle, during the sessions, Lynne originally had thirteen songs for which he could not choose titles at first, hence the monikers Boogies Nos 1 and 2. The remaining eleven presumably found more conventional names more quickly.

5. 'Kuiama'

At over eleven minutes, this was the longest track they ever recorded, and with its anti-war message, certainly the weightiest track in terms of meaning, if not one of the most profound numbers in their whole catalogue. Bevan called it Lynne's 'protest song', adding that Lynne was 'not really into that sort of thing'. Lynne himself said it was his favourite on the album, and although it might make sombre listening when compared to the more well-remembered 'Roll Over Beethoven', several fans' polls and comments online have agreed with this verdict. Musically, it is a gentle piece, with verses and instrumental sections from piano, strings, and lead guitar alternating or combining. As this section reaches a crescendo, it ends on a few stirring orchestral notes and a sound perhaps meant to convey that of an aeroplane or helicopter coming in to land, signifying eventual escape to a better world—or alternately, a grand, dramatic, even apocalyptic close to the album, in the style of the final chord on The Beatles' 'A Day in the Life'.

Like Bob Dylan, Lynne was not often one for explaining the meanings of his songs and music, leaving listeners to draw their own conclusions, particularly after the first few albums. In an interview in 1981, he explained that he found it very hard to talk about his songs: 'What they mean and stuff.... I don't really know what they mean myself sometimes. I just write them and if it looks nice, I like it'.[5]

He did, however, give an interview when *ELO 2* was released, explaining the basic story in the song. Kuiama, a little girl with a Vietnamese name, wanders around the streets in her homeland, a war zone, searching desperately for her parents while she sees nothing but scenes of bloodshed, desolation, and horror. At length she finds a soldier, who tells her sadly that he has shot them both dead. He tries to explain that he was under orders, governed by 'rules with no reason', and taught to kill because he owes a duty to his Fatherland. Sent away to earn his living with a gun in his hand, he had no choice.

On the American *Olé ELO* compilation album, initial pressings had the full eleven-minute version, with later pressings and reissues having a slightly edited nine-minute version. *The Early Years* compilation includes as the final track the five-minute-thirty-second version of '10538 Overture' (cited thus on the track listing), followed by a short pause and then a 'hidden track', a five-minute instrumental version of 'Kuiama'. The same album is on Spotify, where the track is listed as 'Kuiama—Instrumental TV Version', even though '10538 Overture' comes first, as on the CD.

Bonus Tracks

6. 'Showdown'

As far as original British releases went, this was their only standalone single, and a No. 12 hit in autumn 1973 (US Cashbox No. 51, Billboard No. 53). It was their last release on the Harvest label under their British contract with EMI Records, signed in 1970. In America, they had always been signed to United Artists Records, and the track thus appeared on the

American issue of *On the Third Day* (see p. 28), their first record on the Warner Brothers label in Britain. In the twenty-first century, it was available on CD reissues of both *ELO 2* and *On the Third Day*.

Few, if any, could have foreseen what looked like a startling change in direction on a song, which in the view of *Face the Music* fanzine was 'simply the best thing ELO had done up to that point'. It owed less to pop or progressive rock and classics and a little more to Motown and Philly soul, especially with Richard's funky synths and its echoes of Stevie Wonder's recent hit 'Superstition'. The group had been rehearsing 'I Heard It through the Grapevine' for fun, and felt Lynne always intended to write something similar one day. He admitted he had 'this thing going in [his] mind, which didn't sound like ELO at all'—an attempt to fuse Tamla rhythms with classical strings, and adding more light and shade instead of just cellos scraping away all the time. The result, for some reason originally called 'Bev's Trousers', was eventually named 'Showdown', 'which sounded more like a black American record'. An earlier recording, about five seconds shorter but otherwise very similar, appeared on *Early Years*.

In September 1974, while being interviewed on a radio station in New York City, John Lennon said that if The Beatles had stayed together, they would be sounding like ELO, 'Son of Beatles', and that 'Showdown' sounded like 'a beautiful combination' of 'Grapevine' and Lou Christie's 'Lightning Strikes', 'with a little "Walrus" underneath.'

On a subsequent tour of the States, Lynne had almost lost his voice, and one afternoon, he asked Michael de Albuquerque if he would mind taking lead vocal on some of the songs on the show that night, including 'Showdown'. The bassist was surprised to find that towards the end, one line read 'it's unreal, the suffering'—he had always assumed Lynne was singing, 'It's surreal, this submarine'.

7. 'In Old England Town' (instrumental)

Released as the B-side of 'Showdown', this opens with a few seconds of what sounds like a tremolo effect on an amplified guitar chord, with synthesiser playing the vocal melody line and the guitar solo given more prominence. Another version, minus the first few seconds, but otherwise identical, was released on the *Harvest Showdown* compilation, under its early working title of 'King Henry VIII's B*ll*cks'.

8. 'Baby I Apologise'

Completely out of character with the rest of the album, this was a chirpy, poppy number recorded in June 1973, sounding like a Lynne solo demo with multi-tracked vocals, piano, Hammond organ, and handclaps—or possibly a fun moment in the studio featuring just Lynne and Tandy, never meant for release. Lynne said that it was 'rather silly but has some nice chords'. Another theory is that it was recorded as a demo, which he might have thought suitable for pitching to other artists as a potential single. When it was uploaded on YouTube, one tongue-in-cheek comment read: 'I really appreciate your posting of Kermit the Frog's lost single'.

9. 'Auntie'

This was the original working title for the song that became 'Ma-Ma-Ma-Belle', a single from the subsequent album *On the Third Day*. Two early versions are presented here, the first being a one-minute instrumental using guitar, bass, and drums on the intro, first verse, and first chorus to see how the dual guitars would work, and the second is a four-minute rough run-through with vocal. *Early ELO* contained two almost identical early run-throughs of the song, one called 'Auntie' and the other 'My Woman'.

10. 'Mambo (Dreaming of 4000)'

An early version of a song that would appear in finished form on the third album later that year.

11. 'Everyone's Born to Die'

This features the 'electric nucleus' of the group (Lynne, Bevan, Tandy, and de Albuquerque) and Marc Bolan of T. Rex (a friend of Lynne since the latter's Idle Race days) on joint lead guitar and maybe also backing vocals. The slow, mournful song, with a basic message of 'nothing lasts forever', is reminiscent of *Blonde On Blonde*-era Bob Dylan, with the Hammond organ effect sounding rather like 'One of Us Must Know'. At the end of the song is about a minute of jamming on a twelve-bar blues sequence, led by piano and guitar. It bears no relation to the song, which can be heard in its standalone glory as one of the bonus tracks on *On the Third Day* and was evidently a little bit of musical fun while the tape was still running. According to ELO archivist Rob Caiger, the absence of a chorus might have been the reason why Lynne did not put strings on it and left it unreleased for so long.

12. 'Roll Over Beethoven'

Apart from Lynne and Bevan going 'ho ho ho ho' over the initial Fifth Symphony intro and a little bit of vocal tomfoolery at the end—with Lynne clearly saying 'C'mon, Ludwig!' during the coda a few seconds before the end—it hardly differs from the finished version.

The Lost Planet

The bonus album that was issued as Disc 2 of the thirtieth anniversary boxed set (which is no longer available) includes three numbers from BBC sessions and three recorded with former Move vocalist Carl Wayne. The latter had made several solo singles since leaving the group in 1970, but without success. Not a songwriter himself, he was longing to record something more soulful than the lightweight pop with which he had been presented so far. Don Arden, who had formerly managed The Move and was now working in a similar capacity for ELO and Wizzard, had just taken Wayne on himself and suggested Lynne might be able to provide him with the right material. Lynne promptly wrote two songs to order and reworked 'Momma' (altering the title slightly in the process), finishing them off on the day of the session in their minibus as they went from Birmingham to AIR Studios. As with 'Everyone's Born to Die' above, it was just the 'electric nucleus' participating without the string players. Yet Wayne was delighted to be working with old friends again, and as they arrived, he handed round bottles of white wine. The tracks were not completed and have a slightly demo-like feel, and the intention to add strings at a later date was there. All the tapes were assumed lost until 2003, when a search for bonus tracks began and everything in the vaults was checked.

1. 'Brian Matthew introduces ELO/From the Sun to the World (Boogie No. 1)'

The BBC Radio presenter announces a track from the album specially recorded for a BBC session, a faithful recreation of the studio version but about a minute shorter, fading out at the end on a fast piano and violin break.

2. 'Momma'

The second BBC session track, sounding almost identical to the studio version—and the same length.

3. 'Roll Over Beethoven' (single version) (Chuck Berry)

The four-minute-thirty-five-second version, as heard regularly on radio at the time and many times since as a golden oldie.

4. 'Showdown' (Take 1)

There is very little difference between this and the more familiar single edit, except that this is about fifteen seconds longer, thanks to a little high-pitched synthesiser doodling at the end, which carries on for about fifteen seconds after the other instruments have faded out.

5. 'Your World'

The first of the songs featuring Wayne on vocal is a soulful impassioned song of defiance with some suitably forceful guitar in the introduction and break to match.

6. 'Get a Hold of Myself' (Take 2)

Like the foregoing, this is another strong vocal performance from Wayne, with a mid-tempo, quite funky backing in places. As Lynne said, these three tracks were never finished, least of all this one, where the instruments suddenly stop in thin air.

7. 'Mama' (Take 1)

A slight alteration in spelling, and at five minutes long, this is a couple of minutes shorter than the version on the original release. It is interesting to compare the voices of Wayne and Lynne, and here the instrumentation is slightly different, with piano and occasional synthesiser supplying the chords and notes that had been played on strings, thus replacing the more classical stylings of ELO's version. There had been plans for it to be released as a single once completed with the addition of strings, and according to an interview with Bevan, Richard Harris had also shown interest in recording it.

8. 'Wilf's solo' (instrumental) (Wilf Gibson)

A three-minute instrumental recording, broken about halfway through by a little studio chatter, written (or improvised) by the violinist himself. It had originally been intended for inclusion on *On the Third Day* as part of 'In the Hall of The Mountain King'.

9. 'Roll Over Beethoven' (BBC session) (Chuck Berry)

The fourth different (well, slightly different) version of the song on this collection is the seven-and-a-half-minute version, similar to the one used on *Flashback* almost three decades later, but played slightly faster and about ten seconds shorter.

On the Third Day

UK:	Released December 1973, Warner Bros, did not chart
US:	Released March 1974, United Artists, No. 31 (Cashbox), No. 52 (Billboard)
Current edition:	Legacy/Sony CD
Personnel:	Jeff Lynne: vocals, guitars Bev Bevan: drums, percussion Richard Tandy: piano, Moog, clavinet, Wurlitzer electric piano Colin Walker, Mike Edwards: cellos Michael de Albuquerque: bass guitar, backing vocals Wilf Gibson, Mik Kaminski: violin

Walker and Gibson both left during the recording of the album, the latter being replaced by Kaminski, and they were not credited on the sleeve of the original release. 'Cellist Ted Blight', who was credited alongside Edwards, was a figment of Lynne's imagination.

Recorded at De Lane Lea Studios and Air Studios, London, April–May 1973

Produced by Jeff Lynne

After two albums of relatively experimental material, the third found Lynne concentrating on shorter, more commercial numbers, a step away from the prog-rock field and closer into the rock/pop mainstream. Years later, he said this album was one of his favourites: 'It sounds so sweet, so very innocent. It just has the two cellos and one violin on it, that's all there is in the orchestral department'. The first half, in terms of the original vinyl release, was an extended suite of four pieces segued together, while the second half was made up of standalone numbers.

The American (but not the British) issue included 'Showdown', which in Britain had been their last release on the Harvest label under their EMI contract before they moved to Warner Brothers and subsequently Jet (a new label founded by their manager Don Arden). The 2006 CD reissue from Legacy/Sony/BMG includes 'Showdown' plus five bonus tracks. Most of the sound on the album reverted to a fusion of cello-dominated rock, but this time, all tracks were kept to a reasonable length with only one exceeding six minutes. In his own words, Jeff was aiming 'to make music that was melodic and different'.

The interlinked tracks on side one, without breaks in between, were a tentative concept loosely based around Biblical themes; these themes were connected to the formation of the land and the seas on the third day in the Old Testament and Jesus arising from the dead in the New. To take The Beatles analogy a stage further, some listeners may find echoes here of the extended cycle of different songs that take up most of side two of the original group's *Abbey Road*.

Tracks

1. 'Ocean Breakup/King of the Universe'

Opens with portentous strings and synths, with dreamy vocals coming in after two minutes or so. The general feeling is that of a brief overture, followed by a song—or rather brief lyric—about a 'golden sunrise', overshadowed by a 'tragic daydream'. The intro of the 'Ocean Breakup' portion has a high-toned Morse code signal played on keyboard below the synthesiser and strings in the left channel, repeating the code for 'ELO' (dot/dot-dash-dot-dot/dash-dash-dash).

2. 'Bluebird is Dead'

This presents the mournful tale of a man who, in Lynne's words, is talking to someone (probably his girlfriend) who is dead as he cannot come to terms with her death. A rather Lennon-esque vocal gives way to a more spirited instrumental break with keyboards underpinning a guitar solo played backwards.

3. 'Oh No Not Susan'

A similarly downbeat song, this tells the story of a rich heiress living at a stately home with everything money can buy, but to whom material goods mean nothing. Appropriately mournful violin and cellos play around the vocal, and for the last thirty seconds, a synth and faster drumbeat lead into a reprise of the baroque intro before the next track begins. Lynne is heard clearly singing 'they just don't mean a fucking thing' in the last verse, a line that was bowdlerised for obvious reasons on the lyrics printed on the album sleeve.

4. 'New World Rising/Ocean Breakup'

This brings a more upbeat feel, both in the washes of synth and strings and in the more optimistic lyric about a 'new dawn, smiling down the world'. With an echo of the opening track, it makes a neat conclusion to what was originally side one of the record.

5. 'Showdown' (see under *ELO 2*, bonus tracks)

6. 'Daybreaker'

Side two of the original album is a more upbeat affair than the first. Lynne originally wrote this rousing synthesiser and strings instrumental for Birmingham Town Hall as he felt that when the group returned to play in their home town, they needed a really powerful new tune. A bombastic intro flows smoothly into a vigorous tune with baroque echoes that suggest the influence of Bach or Handel at their most spirited, with a snippet of Emerson, Lake, and Palmer thrown in. There is even a brief quote from the verse of the much-covered Robert Knight/Love Affair oldie 'Everlasting Love'. The last twenty seconds sound more or less like another track, with soft ambient keyboard sounds that also form part of the bonus track 'Interludes'.

7. 'Ma-Ma-Ma-Belle'

The single, with 'Oh No Not Susan' on the B-side, was a No. 22 hit in Britain. In America, it failed to chart until a radio disc jockey began promoting 'Daybreaker' on the B-side, giving them a lowly hit at No. 87. It was easily the most instantly commercial moment on the album, and while Lynne regularly flirted with rock 'n' roll and rockabilly, this and 'Do Ya' (see p. 43) were the closest to the world of air guitar music in the entire ELO catalogue. Rob Mackie of *Sounds* called it the nearest thing they had ever done to 'a hefty rock record, and the cellos thump away like Dumbo on heat'. An infectiously simple chord sequence on guitar and suitably raw cellos provide the backdrop for a driving four minutes, with lyrics that mean little—not that it matters. The song has something of the feel of The Rolling Stones' 'Brown Sugar' without saxophones, of Free's 'All Right Now', and also of Bad Company's 'Can't Get Enough' (the latter having been recorded and released at almost the same time). It has been pointed out that the opening chords are not that far removed from those of Mott the Hoople's 'Jerkin' Crocus', a track on the album *All the Young Dudes*. The single is slightly edited, fading a little earlier and thus about thirty seconds shorter than the album version. It also has a few seconds of a rising note on the strings (a sample from the next track, 'Dreaming of 4000', with the tape run backwards and heavily phased) after the second chorus. This was edited out of the album version, but subsequent compilations use the album version without this interlude.

Marc Bolan played guitar on earlier studio run-throughs of this and the next track, although sources differ as to whether his contributions were used on the final versions.

In America, it was also used on the B-side of 'Livin' Thing' in 1976 (see p. 43), partly to help promote the earlier albums and the more recent *Olé ELO* compilation.

Although not one of their major hits on either side of the Atlantic, it became a regular staple of their stage show throughout the years, generally played near the end of the set as a rousing 'get up and dance' number. During the early 1980s, it was played as part of a medley with their two other heaviest rockers, 'Do Ya' and 'Rockaria!' Although the standalone version is not included on either of their live CDs, performances can be seen and heard on several DVDs, which reveal the live version to have been about forty seconds longer. The arrangement varied slightly from one show to another—sometimes they retained the rising note after the second chorus. Also, basically where the recorded version fades out—or strictly speaking cross-fades into 'Dreaming of 4000'—the opening chords are repeated a few times, ascending a little in pitch each time, with violin played over the top, after which the song comes to an end with a slower and more ornate crescendo using guitar chords and the string players. The effect of the rising pitch gives an effect similar to that which might be heard by playing the vinyl record and manually speeding it up.

8. 'Dreaming of 4000'

For the most part, this is an urgently paced number beginning with brisk lead guitar, which gives way to a slower verse with more or less abstract lyrics about a 'saviour of the night' and 'the dawning of the daybreak'. There are several dramatic changes of pace and mood, with suitably spirited interplay between cello, violin, and moog, leading to a dramatic crescendo—all within only five minutes. Initial British pressings mistitled it as 'I'm Only Dreaming' on the label.

9. 'In the Hall of the Mountain King' (Edvard Grieg, credited on album as 'Traditional, arranged by ELO' and CD as 'Arranged by ELO')

The only classical piece they ever covered on a studio recording, this was originally composed by Norwegian composer Edvard Grieg for *Peer Gynt*, a play by Henrik Ibsen, in 1876. In six and a half minutes, they take a few minor liberties with the arrangement, while preserving the light and shade of the original. A short, echo-soaked peaceful harpsichord intro crossfades into the sounds of wind and softly shimmering violins, then the main theme is played quietly on strings and synths until a blast of drums takes it in to top gear with the main theme on cellos. About four minutes in, it changes briefly into a piece of violin music, part Celtic dance and part Gypsy jazz. Forty seconds later, there is a reprise of the main theme, following Grieg's original in gathering pace until the closing crescendo.

The group briefly considered it as a third single, either in its own right or as a double A-side with 'Showdown', but then decided against it, mainly as they did not wish to be seen as a band relying heavily on cover versions. Sometimes they referred to it as 'In the Hole of the Stuffed Parrot'. One of the most popular nineteenth-century classics, it has also been recorded by The Who, Madness, Erasure, and the Brighouse & Rastrick Brass Band.

Marc Bolan and Electric Light Orchestra

Marc Bolan had made an impromptu appearance with them on stage at Watford Town Hall in April 1973 for a fifteen-minute encore of 'Roll Over Beethoven'. For years, it was commonly accepted that he played dual lead guitar alongside Lynne on 'Showdown', 'Ma-Ma-Ma-Belle', and 'Dreaming of 4000', but that he was uncredited on the sleeve for contractual reasons. Recent research through record company archives has confirmed that this was incorrect. He was never on 'Showdown', although Lynne did borrow Bolan's 1953 Firebird guitar for the session. As regards the other two songs, Bolan probably played only on the unreleased versions, which were later issued as bonus tracks. His presence might have created contractual issues regarding an official release for 'Everyone's Born to Die', although Bolan and T. Rex were at that time releasing records on the T. Rex label through EMI, who owned the Harvest label on which the first two ELO albums appeared. However, it was not uncommon for groups to employ other high-profile friends as guests on their studio recordings, and keep it quiet in order to circumvent legal difficulties.

Bonus Tracks

Not counting 'Showdown', which might be regarded as an extra as far as the British (but not American) release is concerned, the remastered 2006 CD reissue has five bonus tracks.

10. 'Auntie' (two versions)

11. 'Mambo (Dreaming of 4000)'

Both the above are musically the same as the bonus tracks on *ELO 2* above

12. 'Everyone's Born to Die'

As per the version on *ELO 2* above, although minus the unrelated jam session that follows the song itself, thus making it about a minute shorter. Although recorded without strings—Lynne might have had ideas to complete it with violin and cellos—and therefore would have sounded rather out of place on any contemporary group release, more than forty years later, it still sounds magnificent, a powerful performance and composition that should have not been left to languish unheard for so long.

13. 'Interludes'

Three and a half minutes or so of random doodling on keyboard and strings are broken up with muffled studio chatter, plus several stops and starts. The first part sounds loosely like a variation on pieces by Erik Satie, with keyboards joined later on by the sound of a violin being plucked instead of played with a bow. About twenty sections of the latter section were integrated into the end of 'Daybreaker', or else added on as an 'interlude' afterwards, as it sounds more like a completely different short track.

Eldorado: A Symphony by the Electric Light Orchestra

UK:	Released October 1974, Warner Bros
US:	Released September 1974, United Artists, No. 16 (Cashbox and Billboard)
Current edition:	Legacy/Sony CD
Personnel:	Jeff Lynne: vocals, guitars, bass guitar, Moog Bev Bevan: drums, percussion Richard Tandy: piano, Moog, clavinet, Wurlitzer electric piano, guitar, backing vocals Colin Walker, Mike Edwards: cellos Michael de Albuquerque: bass guitar, backing vocals (he left before recording sessions were complete) Mik Kaminski: violin Peter Forbes-Robertson: spoken word Louis Clark: orchestral and choral arrangements

Recorded at De Lane Lea Studios, London, February–August 1974
Produced by Jeff Lynne

Eldorado, the fourth ELO album, was the first that Lynne wrote entirely on his own, coming up with every song from start to finish in one week. From now on, all subsequent albums would consist entirely of his material. With its subtitle, forty-piece orchestra, and choir, and concept theme based on the experiences of a Walter Mitty-like character living in a fantasy world (dreaming he is high on a hill in the mythical land of Eldorado), it was probably in a sense their most classical-sounding album. Lynne was thrilled to hear a full orchestra playing his music after several years of merely multi-tracking a violin and a couple of cellos.

Although some fans consider it arguably their best ever, it was ironically released at a time when the group were experiencing a lull in their British fortunes as far as singles and album chart success went—yet they found that their tours of America were paying off. This was the one that helped to make them stars across the Atlantic, partly as a result of a sleeve design based on a still from *The Wizard of Oz* (a design that the group initially hated until the significance was pointed out to them), and it was also unquestionably a new high for them. Roy Wood said around the time of its release that it was the best album he had heard since *Sergeant Pepper's Lonely Hearts Club Band.*

Shortly before it appeared in Britain, Lynne said in an interview that they were only interested in making albums:

> We're not a singles band but if you have a hit single there's always people who think you're a singles group. Over here for the majority of people if you haven't got a record in the charts it means you're not doing anything, but that's a pathetic attitude. But if the record company say they're going to release a single what can you do about it? You can't argue. I could write horrible hit singles, I'm sure I could but I don't want to do it.... I like something a bit deeper than pop clichés.[6]

While the album was being recorded, Lynne faced some difficulty with members of the Musicians' Union who had been hired to play the string parts under the direction of Louis Clark, who was responsible for the arrangements. As they were being paid by the hour, union rules would not allow them to play for any additional time, regardless of whether the work was incomplete or not. Their hour was up during the sessions for one track, so some of them stopped playing on time, put their instruments away, and slammed the cases shut. The affected take was kept and used, with the noise being mixed down until it was inaudible even on the finest audio equipment that the 1970s could offer. However, his frustration with such practices led Lynne to vow that all subsequent ELO albums would be recorded outside Britain, mainly at Musicland Studios, Munich, where musicians took more pride in their craft than in watching the clock. 'Nobody's Child' was the track generally identified by those with sharp ears as the one with the slamming cases, though some listeners think it may have been the title track or 'Eldorado Finale'.

Tracks

1. 'Eldorado Overture'

A two-minute strings and synth instrumental that sounds in turn quite spacey and ambient, and to some extent rather like the musical soundtrack of an old 1950s movie. Its brief spoken prologue introduces us to 'the dreamer, the unwoken fool' as it segues seamlessly into the album's best-known track.

2. 'Can't Get It Out of My Head'

A single on both sides of the Atlantic, it failed in Britain, but reached No. 9 (Billboard) and No. 14 (Cashbox) in America. The belated limited edition release, pressed mainly for the jukebox trade, reached No. 52 in Britain in 1979, although some maintain that in official chart statistics, it should be counted under sales for the four-track EP released in December 1978 to promote the *Three Light Years* boxed set, which reached the Top 40. There is a slightly 'Imagine'-like feel to it, especially in the hero's wistful lament for a way of his old dreamland, 'my whole world is gone for dead'.

Sometimes considered one of the best ELO ballads ever, Lynne wrote it as a challenge to criticism of his songwriting from father Phil, a classical music lover who had imparted his passion to his son as a boy and had told him that the trouble with his songs was that they had 'got no bloody tune'. Lynne Jr's response was to prove that he could write something with a beautiful classically inspired melody, and promptly sat down in his parents' front room in Shard End, Birmingham, to prove his point. It may also have inspired him to use a full orchestra on the song, and subsequently album, instead of relying on the overdubbed work of two cellists and one violinist.

Interviewed on VH1's *Storytellers*, Lynne said that the lyrics were 'about a man who was dreaming, sees this vision of loveliness and wakes up and finds that he's actually a clerk working in a bank', with no chance of doing any of the wonderful things that he had imagined. Among cover versions was one by Jonathan King, recorded under one of his aliases, 'One Hundred Ton and a Feather', released in 1977.

3. 'Boy Blue'

Released as a second single in America only, it failed to chart. It is introduced by a short string quartet fanfare, arranged on a variation of 'The Prince of Denmark's March', composed *c.* 1700 by Jeremiah Clarke and often mistakenly attributed to his contemporary Henry Purcell. Lynne said that it was a celebration of 'an all-conquering hero from the middle ages', it is a busy track with plenty going on within the five minutes—flourishes of rock guitar, fiddle, and strings, touches of choral vocals, and a very catchy hook on the chorus.

4. 'Laredo Tornado'

A slower, more moody piece makes use of plenty of echo on the vocals, snarling guitar, and almost funky synth work. Towards the end, there is a brief almost a cappella section, with only drums behind the harmony vocals. The lyrics were intended to be 'kind of a protest dream about the proliferation of concrete'.

5. 'Poor Boy (The Greenwood)'

This brings a change of pace with more up-tempo fare. There are references in the lyrics to Maid Marian and Robin Hood robbing the rich to help the poor, plus a few speed-ups and slow-downs supported well by the strings in all their glory, with a feast of infectious hooks along the way. The closing thirty seconds or so almost amount to a dazzling contest between strings and choir of Wagnerian proportions.

6. 'Mister Kingdom'

Another nod to John Lennon comes in this atmospheric, haunting song, with something of a similarity to The Beatles' 'Across the Universe' in the melody. It ends in a sweeping bombastic strings finale.

7. 'Nobody's Child'

Preceded by another short 'The Prince of Denmark's March' quote, this is almost a jazzy slow shuffle, with something of a Ray Charles feel.

8. 'Illusions in G Major'

A sparkling example of Lynne's sure touch at writing great Chuck Berry pastiches in the manner of Status Quo. He referred to it as 'a jolly name-dropping rocker'—how many other songs namecheck poems by Keats and Browning (Clifford T. Ward's 'Home Thoughts from Abroad' apart) or tunes written by the Rolling Stones and Leonard Cohen—and this is British rock 'n' roll at its mid-1970s best. The classical-style title conceals a song that starts off as a twelve-bar and then introduces an unexpected minor chord towards the end of the verse. Full-tilt strings, brass, and a scorching fuzztone guitar break make this arguably the album's most infectious moment. Despite the obvious similarity to their version of 'Roll Over Beethoven', one can imagine that seven or eight years later, when it was not unusual for three or four album tracks to be issued as singles, this might have had more of a chance of charting than 'Can't Get It Out of My Head', on which it appeared as the B-side.

9. 'Eldorado'

The title track is another dreamy ballad, sounding almost like something out of one of the more restrained not-quite-finale moments from a 1930s or 1940s Hollywood musical, with lush strings and a crescendo of choral vocals to the end behind Lynne's singing. After the adrenaline rush of the preceding song, it is very effective. It is followed by a ninety-second 'Eldorado Finale', a short reprise of the opening track.

Bonus Tracks

10. 'Eldorado Instrumental Medley'

Eight minutes' worth of music threaded into an instrumental, which connect the overture, finale, and most of the songs in between into one extended piece. With the skilful balance of light and shade, the concept resembles the Gilbert & Sullivan overtures for the Savoy Operas, which used to reprise a brief snatch of almost every song.

11. 'Dark City'

A forty-second early demo for the number that became 'Laredo Tornado'.

Face the Music

UK:	Released November 1975
US:	Released September 1975, United Artists, No. 13 (Cashbox); No. 8 (Billboard)
Current edition:	Legacy/Sony CD
Personnel:	Jeff Lynne: vocals, guitars Bev Bevan: drums, percussion, backing vocals, spoken intro (backwards) Richard Tandy: piano, Moog, clavinet, Wurlitzer electric piano, guitar, backing vocals Hugh McDowell, Melvyn Gale: cellos Kelly Groucutt: bass guitar, backing vocals, lead on *Down Home Town* Mik Kaminski: violin Ellie Greenwich, Susan Collins, Nancy O'Neill, Margaret Raymond: backing vocals Louis Clark: orchestral and choral arrangements

Recorded at Musicland Studios, Munich, May–June 1975
Produced by Jeff Lynne
Engineered by Mack Reinhold

The group's fifth studio album was the first to be recorded outside England following their disagreeable experiences with the Musicians' Union while they were making *Eldorado.* It was also the first to be released on the Jet label, launched the previous year by manager Don Arden in Britain and by former Warner Bros manager Des Brown in America. Although, like its predecessor, it did not chart in Britain until released as part of a three-album package some three years later, it spawned two Top 40 singles in their home land. It is regarded as one of their most adventurous albums with its juxtaposition of classics and rock.

Tracks

1. 'Fire on High'

Lynne reached a new high, musically speaking, with the opening track on this fifth album—a very adventurous instrumental work of great contrasts. The start sums up a chilling atmosphere redolent of vintage sci-fi movies, a feeling of approaching menace, and a musical setting that, in the first seventy-five seconds, owes something to the work of Schoenberg and Wagner, and brief snatches from the 'Hallelujah Chorus' from Handel's *Messiah.*

The short spoken passage is indecipherable at first, but when played backwards, it supposedly reveals Bevan saying 'The music is reversible, but time is not. Turn back, turn back, turn back, turn back…' It was Lynne's tongue-in-cheek response to assertions from members of a fundamentalist American Christian organisation, which stated that Lynne had added Satanic messages to 'Eldorado' that were only audible when played backwards; this group either had too much time on their hands or an over-vivid imaginations. They claimed that the line 'Here it comes, another lonely day, playing the game. I'll sail away, on a voyage of no return to see' actually said something along the lines of 'He is the nasty one—Christ you're infernal—It is said we're dead men—Everyone who has the mark will live'. The group were quick to deny any such thing, Lynne saying that, as far as he was concerned, he worked quite hard enough 'getting the lyrics going forwards' and it would be impossible for him to write lines that conveyed any meaningful message when played in reverse. These backwards 'messages' were nothing less than a calculated leg-pull for the conspiracy theory lovers. Any listener keen to test this is advised to seek out a copy of the American Super Bit Mapping collector's edition 24kt gold CD reissue from 1995, on which this segment, run forwards, can be found as a hidden track. Alternatively, at the time of writing, somebody has helpfully posted the relevant part of the track forwards and backwards on YouTube.

After this, a more dominant orchestral motif takes over, drums enter, and it all gives way to a baroque-sounding interlude on keyboards, morphing into a stately, slow piece reminiscent of Elton John's 'Funeral for a Friend', with lead guitar and violin alternately taking solos. At almost three minutes in, crisp acoustic guitars, drums (with a touch of phasing), and slightly jazzy strings come in. With the changes of mood and tempo, there is a good deal going on, and near the end it takes on an almost disco rhythm until the final orchestral crescendo.

2. 'Waterfall'

This ethereal, dreamy love song opens with strings and a plaintive, George Harrison-like guitar sound, with the combination of instruments reminiscent of The Beatles' 'Something' in parts. Gentle piano chords and vocals suggest a hint of Freddie Mercury, with a backdrop of muted choral vocals and swirling strings, and drums coming in at the first chorus. A sturdy instrumental bridge suggests a new departure into classical music-influenced horizons before a return to the song with the introduction repeated on strings and enhanced by the backing vocals until a gentle fade.

3. 'Evil Woman'

The main hit single (No. 10 in Britain and America) was the track that restored their fortunes as a hit singles name at home. The song allegedly took Lynne about six minutes to write, under the pressure of realising that he needed a single on the album—this being the man who had not long before lambasted 'horrible hit singles'—which he did while waiting for the others to arrive at the studio one day. After a deceptively mellow fifteen-second prelude on strings, edited from the version released as a single, comes a series of four dramatic chords, a combination of strings, piano, and tinkling on the cymbals, with the opening vocal phrase over the top. A phrase is played twice on piano, then joined by the rhythm section and funky electric rhythm guitar, which lead into the song. It fitted in very well with the prevailing mood of rock acts putting one foot into disco territory during that same era, notably recent Top 10 hits from The Bee Gees ('Jive Talkin'') and David Bowie ('Golden Years'). The strings in particular show something of a Philadelphia soul influence. Another interesting point comes a few seconds before the last verse, where the strings run backwards—a sample taken from 'Nightrider', the following track—and the backing vocals, not credited at the time of original release, are by a quartet, including renowned American songwriter Ellie Greenwich.

Lynne added a nod to The Beatles in the line, 'a hole in my head where the rain comes in', a tribute of sorts to 'Fixing a Hole' on *Sergeant Pepper's Lonely Hearts Club Band*. The chord sequence is also not a million miles removed from Dylan's 'All Along the Watchtower'.

4. 'Nightrider'

Another of those deceptively simple-sounding songs with a very intricate arrangement, this goes through several changes in just over four minutes, from a plaintive keyboard intro to a more forceful chorus, with some dreamy, other-worldly strings along the way, all coming to a peaceful conclusion. Groucutt takes lead vocal on the second verse. It was the second single off the album in Britain, but it failed to chart despite being featured as a new release on *Top of the Pops* in the week of issue.

5. 'Poker'

This is the album's most hard-rocking moment, opening with a Status Quo-like guitar riff and some frenetic, bubbling Emerson, Lake, and Palmer-style synthesisers. A fast-paced vocal joins in for the first verse, then ninety seconds in, a slower, more mellow section takes over for a few seconds before it speeds up to the frantic opening pace again. There is also a short section based on a motif of descending notes, played on guitar and cellos, which have something of the flavour of the recurring riff that forms the backbone of Led Zeppelin's 'Kashmir'. The lyrics allude vaguely to a card game, with their references to jokers and high cards that call the tune.

6. 'Strange Magic'

The third British single, a No. 38 hit in Britain and No. 14 in America, is a comparatively simple number. A short orchestral interlude starts the number before an ethereal lead guitar section, played by Tandy this time—again bringing the style of George Harrison to mind—leads it in to an uncomplicated, dreamy love song.

7. 'Down Home Town'

ELO went to the heart of deepest Nashville on this song, which is oddly out of character, but nonetheless very effective. The first few seconds feature more reverse-tape sounds, which were beginning to become a habit by now, before it turns into a country hoedown with fiddle and a twang in the lead vocal, featuring Groucutt for a change. Female backing vocals contribute with lines about wishing they were 'in the land of Dixie'.

8. 'One Summer Dream'

Considering the size of their back catalogue, ELO recorded hardly any songs that might be considered suitable candidates for the average *Summer: The Ultimate Collection* compilation album. This is one such number. A laid-back affair with lush strings, Lynne sounds relaxed as he almost croons the words, with a deep echoing choral vocal section, repeating the title at intervals. One can only assume it was recorded at the height of a hot summer—the very antithesis, one assumes, to the wet season in Germany two years later, which helped to inspire 'Concerto for a Rainy Day' on side three of *Out of the Blue* (see p. 49).

Bonus Tracks

9. 'Fire on High Intro'

This early version is shorter than the finished track. With the same four-note motif on piano dominant and lacking the overdubs, it is clearly a work-in-progress recording.

10. 'Evil Woman'

Another earlier version, this is nearly a minute longer than the finished recording, with an extra verse that was discarded; this version is also without the strings.

11. 'Strange Magic'

The single edit, without the short orchestral introduction, thus losing almost one minute from the album version in the process.

12. 'Waterfall'

An instrumental mix, this is the backing track and it is around the same length as the finished vocal version.

A New World Record

UK:	Released November 1976, Jet/United Artists, No. 6
US:	Released September 1976, United Artists, No. 5 (Billboard), No. 10 (Cashbox)
Current edition:	Legacy/Sony CD

Personnel:
Jeff Lynne: vocals, guitars, electric piano
Bev Bevan: drums, percussion
Richard Tandy: piano, clavinet, Moog, guitar, backing vocals
Hugh McDowell, Melvyn Gale: cellos
Kelly Groucutt: bass guitar, backing vocals
Mik Kaminski: violin
Mary Thomas: operatic vocals (track 3)
Patti Quatro, Brie Brandt, Addie Lee: backing vocals
Louis Clark: orchestral and choral arrangements

Recorded at Musicland Studios, Munich, July 1976
Produced by Jeff Lynne

In the British market above all, and the first to feature the distinctive ELO logo designed by John Kosh (former Creative Director for The Beatles' Apple Records), this sixth album was the record that completely turned their chart fortunes around. After their first two had only made the Top 40 and the next three failed to appear in the lists at all, this entered at No. 10 in its first week, reaching a peak position of No. 6 several months later. It was kept alive by three Top 10 singles—'Livin' Thing', 'Rockaria!', and 'Telephone Line'—and stayed there for exactly 100 weeks over the next three years. In America, 'Do Ya' was a single instead of 'Rockaria!' It also marked the start of ten unbroken years of Top 10 British albums, excluding boxed sets containing previously issued material. As Lynne said in the notes for the booklet that accompanied the 2006 reissue, 'Going from doing okay for probably three or four years to suddenly being in the big time, it was a strange but great thing.'

Tracks

1. 'Tightrope'

This is generally regarded as one of the group's best tracks that was never released as a single, although it has remained a regular favourite in their stage show. A dignified orchestral intro with deep operatic-cum-choral voices in the background take up the first minute or so, then the violins launch a sonic sizzle, the drums come in, and there is a catchy phrase on electric guitar as it all speeds up and the song fairly rocks—yet it is full of those catchy hooks that proclaim it as honest infectious pop. Then it slows down again for a reprise of the introduction before speeding up yet again.

2. 'Telephone Line'

The third British single (No. 8), also released in America (No. 7, at the time their highest-charting ever there), is called by some one of the best ballads that Lennon and McCartney never wrote. A few electronic beeps open the song, while strings and keyboards offer plenty of light and shade as Lynne sings the story of near-desperation, a caller who laments that nobody is answering and who has no choice but to sit tight and 'let it ring for evermore'. In at least one interview, he hinted that the idea for the lyrics came shortly after he had finished a tour, presumably the North American leg of the *Face the Music* shows, and was thinking about his American girlfriend, Sandi Kapelson, secretary at the Jet Records offices in Los Angeles, whom he married in 1979.

As the first verse begins (with the opening line 'Hello, how are you' on loan from a 1968 hit by The Easybeats of that title), the opening lines have a muted sound as if being sung or heard through the telephone. Lynne had the idea after the master recording had been completed, and this effect was added by the studio engineers in the final stage.

3. 'Rockaria!'

ELO's major contribution to that select list of vocal hits not containing the exact title in the lyrics, the album's second British Top 10 entry (No. 9) (like 'Illusions in G Major' from *Eldorado*), is in Lynne's words 'a tongue-in-cheek look at classical rock', in which he takes what starts as a 12-bar rock 'n' roll song and adds a few twists of his own. The first voice to be heard is that of Welsh opera singer Mary Thomas, with '*Aah, fern, wiet'r in die ferne, man hört man hört die Musik*' ('far, far away, the music is playing')—a line that Lynne sings during the song's bridge before the final verse. Her performance of the line is followed by an apologetic 'Oops!' Lynne recorded her rehearsal take and edited it in afterwards for a joke, although with her approval. This false beginning was retained on the album version, but edited off the British single and on most compilations. On stage, Groucutt used to supply the falsetto part or else allegedly mime to a tape.

The operatic introduction, backed by strings, gave way to a fusillade on drums and searing slide guitar as if The Rolling Stones and Little Richard were taking on the Vienna Philharmonic. The lyrics tell of a sweet little lady who sings like a songbird, who's sweet on Wagner, who'd die for Beethoven, loves the way Puccini lays down a tune, and how Verdi's always 'creepin'' from her room; in the last verse, there is a nod to 'Roll Over Beethoven' in a line about the orchestra playing all Chuck Berry's greatest tunes. After a grand crescendo in the last verse, the whole thing comes to a breathless end in a frenzy of strings and more operatic vocals.

4. 'Mission (A World Record)'

Despite almost being the title track, this remains one of the lesser performances on the album. A gentle song about travelling from a distant place and time, it begins with a distorted spoken message: 'This is Electric Light (these last two words reversed) calling you from Planet Earth'. It then coasts happily, if unadventurously with strings and an interesting, yet slightly out of character funky guitar break along the way.

5. 'So Fine'

This is another early example of ELO's embracing disco with the fizzing violins, 'woo-hoo' backing vocals, and funky rhythm guitar on this song. Lynne had doubtless already been ingesting the Philly soul sound as much as he had the Bee Gees' recent forays into dance music. It also embraces a wonderfully freaky passage about halfway through, with just percussion and what sounds like somebody playing around with the tape; [this was common practice] in the pre-digital days, when records were recorded on old-fashioned magnetic tape on huge plastic reels. The end featured dropping strings in order to segue with the following track. To create this effect, Lynne asked the engineer to switch off the tape machine so the strings could wind down with the slowing of the tape playback, the recording being cut just as the string hit the same note as the first of the violin that began 'Livin' Thing'.

6. 'Livin' Thing'

The first single, peaking at No. 4 in Britain, begins just as the last chord of the previous song comes in on strings and does a quick musical descent on one note. A bouncy tune, a generous helping of backing vocals, soloing violin, pizzicato riff, and sturdy work on the cellos made this a number that was impossible to ignore on the radio. In August 2006, it was named by *Q Magazine* as readers' all-time No. 1 'Guilty Pleasure' single.

Soon after release, it was rumoured that the lyrics were about saving the whales, orgasms, or maybe even abortion. An argument was advanced in favour of the latter because of references in the first verse about sex ('slippin' and slidin', it's magic'), in the second about pregnancy ('this is what you conceived'), and in the third about termination ('so let her go … it's a bad dream'), with the 'livin' thing' being the baby in question. Somewhere, a music journalist and his imagination were evidently getting carried away. Lynne quashed all speculation by affirming that the lyrics were actually about love. He had been dissatisfied with his original lyric, and just before they were due to mix it, he rewrote them in a hurry.

7. 'Above the Clouds'

The shortest track here, at just over two minutes long, is another of those slow, gentle, cosmic songs about 'floating in a sea of dreams', with the only sight being the view above the clouds, accompanied by splendidly mock-classical flourishes and Lynne almost crooning the words. According to *Face the Music* fanzine, the intro showcases his 'seemingly instinctive feel for black music, before settling into a dreamy melody that could have been part of the score of any Hollywood Depression musical, with gloriously lush escapist lyrics to match'.

8. 'Do Ya'

One of the simplest and yet most effective three-chords on guitar intro this side of the early Kinks' hit singles, plus a few bursts of slide guitar and hard-rock vocal harmonies reminiscent of The Sweet at their peak, this was a return to the song Lynne initially recorded with The Move in 1971 as one of the B-side tracks on their last single 'California Man' the following year. The lyrics were among their most remarkable, on a par with John Lennon's more surrealist word-images in 'I am the Walrus', including 'babies dancing in the midnight sun' and 'pigs all sitting watching picture slides'. As an A-side in America, it became their only American hit, albeit a lowly No. 94. When ELO played it on stage, it was received so enthusiastically that they decided to record it again. The Move's version had delivered a mighty blast on rhythm and slide guitars, drums, and no frills. This rereading follows much the same arrangement, apart from a stately finish replacing the galloping drums and an abbreviation of the 'look out baby, there's a train a-comin'' aside on the fadeout on the original, which was condensed to the first two words; however, Lynne retains that razor-sharp guitar sound in all the right places, augmented with strings.

Lynne had always said ELO would never play any Move material onstage as they had no connection to it any more. '[However,] everybody else [notably Todd Rundgren's Utopia] seems to be doing it these days, so we figured we should give it a go—it is Jeff's song, after all,' said Bevan.

> We've found that it's immensely popular onstage. We just hit the opening chords and people go crazy. We kept the arrangement pretty much intact from the original, but I think it's more powerful, especially with the strings, the middle part is really something with the strings undercutting.[7]

9. 'Shangri-La'

ELO being regarded as something of a reincarnation of The Beatles, the dreamy lead guitar coated with strings that start this song could almost be an undiscovered George Harrison or even Eric Clapton track. At over five minutes long, it is the longest, with a dreamy lyric about someone who 'seemed to drift out on the rain that came in somewhere from the blues'; to underline Jeff's inspiration, there is a reference to how '[his] Shangri-La has gone away, faded like the Beatles on "Hey Jude"'. The whole thing dissolves in a glorious cascade of strings and more operatic vocals.

The original Shangri-La was a fictional paradise in *Lost Horizon*, a novel by James Hilton published in 1933. It also inspired and gave its title to what is considered one of Ray Davies's classic songs, an unsuccessful single from The Kinks' 1969 album *Arthur (Or the Decline and Fall of the British Empire*).

Bonus Tracks

The remastered CD (2006) adds six more numbers, five being alternate versions of other tracks on the album.

10. 'Telephone Line' (different vocal)

An earlier, unedited version, with the basic backing track differing slightly from the finished one and without the 'telephone' effect on the first few lines.

11. 'Surrender'

Previously unreleased, this is an uncharacteristically poppy number with a Northern soul or even Motown rhythm, with echoes of The Supremes' 'You Can't Hurry Love' or Martha and the Vandellas' 'Heatwave', with chunky electric rhythm guitar and backing vocals. Written and begun during the album sessions in 1976 for a film soundtrack that never materialised, it was completed in 2006 for the CD reissue and was made available as an iTunes download single, partly to promote the reissue series. Acetates and promotional one-sided 7" singles were pressed in black and blue vinyl, and the few copies that entered circulation immediately became high-priced collectors' items. By coincidence, the person running the pressing plant where they were produced was former ELO cellist Melvyn Gale.

12. 'Tightrope' (instrumental early rough mix)

About ten seconds shorter than the finished version, this omits the spacey sound effects at the beginning of the latter. There is also a break of about five seconds' silence after the slow introduction has finished, and an only just audible count-in of 'three-four' preceding the faster section of what is plainly the backing track.

13. 'Above the Clouds'

Not so much an instrumental version as an incomplete section of the raw orchestra track, being about a minute shorter than the final version and minus guitar and keyboards.

14. 'So Fine' (instrumental early rough mix)

About twenty seconds longer than the finished version, this unedited version of the basic backing track features a slightly truncated introduction (which is mostly vocal on the final one), slight differences to the percussion break about two minutes in, and a single note from the strings at the end, as opposed to the swiftly descending note that leads straight into 'Livin' Thing'.

15. 'Telephone Line' (instrumental) slightly tweaked version.

Once again, this is an unedited version of the basic backing track, albeit around ten seconds longer and minus the flat telephone sound at the start.

Out of the Blue

UK:	Released October 1977, Jet/United Artists (Jet/CBS after change in distribution a few months later), No. 4
US:	Released October 1977, United Artists, No. 4 (Billboard), No. 4 (Cashbox)
Current edition:	Sony/Legacy CD

Personnel: Jeff Lynne: vocals, guitars, electric piano, Moog
Bev Bevan: drums, percussion
Richard Tandy: piano, clavinet, Moog, guitar, backing vocals
Melvyn Gale: piano (track 17 only)
Kelly Groucutt: bass guitar, backing vocals, percussion
Mik Kaminski: violin (tracks 3, 4, 17 only)
Hugh McDowell and Melvyn Gale are credited with cello but did not play on the record, only on the accompanying tour
Louis Clark: orchestral and choral arrangements

Recorded at Musicland Studios, Munich, May–August 1977
Produced by Jeff Lynne

In the days of vinyl (in this particular case black and limited edition blue—and, nearly forty years later, clear as well), this double album was ELO's *magnum opus*, their most ambitious collection, even their equivalent of The Beatles' *Sergeant Pepper*. The head of United Artists in America had originally asked Lynne to record a live double album to emulate the success of Peter Frampton's *Frampton Comes Alive*, but Lynne, no lover of live albums, said he would rather give them a double studio album instead. His offer was accordingly accepted: 'It was terrific that I got the freedom to do it'. He wrote the entire album in three and a half weeks after a sudden burst of creativity while staying in a rented chalet in the Swiss Alps, and it took a further two months to record in Munich. It was the first double album in British music history to generate four Top 20 hit singles and ultimately their most successful.

The iconic sleeve art was inspired partly by the *2001: A Space Odyssey* and *Star Wars* movies, with a spaceship designed by Kosh with art by Shusei Nagaoka, based on the logo that first appeared on the front of *A New World Record*, intended to resemble the space station with a docking shuttle from '2001'. The number JTLA 823 L2 on the shuttle arriving at the space station was the catalogue number for the album's American release. An insert of a cardboard cut-out of the space station and a fold-out poster of each group member were included with initial copies. The space theme was taken further with a huge glowing flying saucer stage set, inside which the group used to play their set each night of the *Out of the Blue* tour or the *Big Night* in North America, from January to October 1978.

All of ELO's albums first released between 1971 and 1986 were remastered and reissued on CD between 2001 and 2007, with bonus tracks. *Out of the Blue* was the only one to make the British album charts on its second coming, doing so in fine style, entering at a peak position of No. 18 and staying on the list for four weeks.

Tracks

1. 'Turn to Stone'

The album's first British single, a British No. 18 hit and the only one not to reach the Top 10, fades in with an exhilarating, busy rush of sound of bubbling Moog riff and crashing cymbals. Lynne's lead vocals have one of their finest moments after the second chorus, with a few seconds of the immortal tongue-twisting phrase, which he always reproduced faithfully in live performances.

2. 'It's Over'

'It's Over' was the final American (but not British) single release from the album, and it reached No. 75. Twelve seconds of strings, evoking the atmosphere of an old Hollywood between-the-wars musical movie—a section from the string work of the coda of 'Mr Blue Sky' reversed—introduce a bittersweet ballad backed mainly by plaintive piano chords and strings. The same title but different song had given Lynne's hero Roy Orbison a British No. 1 in 1964.

3. 'Sweet Talkin' Woman'

The fourth and final British single (No. 6) had been released several months earlier in America, reaching No. 18 (Cashbox) and No. 17 (Billboard). The latter version was about ten seconds shorter, probably the result of an error with the tape machine being run at the wrong speed. It opens with a short quote on violin, the most prominent of Kaminski's rare appearances on the album, supplemented by lead guitar and Moog, a prelude to one of Lynne's most infectious pop tunes with a nod to a dancefloor rhythm. A vocoder is used sparingly to good effect, as is a brief burst of a cappella on the chorus before the song fades out. Originally called 'Dead End Street', Lynne recorded it thus, but then erased the vocal track, altering the lyrics and arrangement. 'A lot of pairs of scissors were used that day,' he noted, although a reference to 'livin' on a dead end street' remains in the third verse. The title might have been altered to avoid confusion with The Kinks' 1966 hit of that title.

Listeners might notice more than a little similarity between the tune and lyrics of the first verse and of a song written by Robert John Lange, 'Do You Believe in Love'—a hit in 1982 for Huey Lewis and The News.

In November 2005, it became the first ELO track to be featured on *Desert Island Discs* as one of the choices of radio and TV presenter Chris Evans, who, a few years later, would play a vital part in persuading Lynne to return to performing live.

4. 'Across the Border'

Train sound effects are followed by strings and synth on a high-energy number driven by keyboards providing their own brass section, becoming part spaghetti western and part mariachi trumpets, recalling memories of the sound on Dave Dee, Dozy, Beaky, Mick & Tich's 1968 No. 1 'The Legend of Xanadu'. A slight touch in the melody line hints at The Beach Boys' 'Heroes and Villains' or, closer to home, Roy Wood's 'Oh What a Shame', and it all comes to a halt with a whoosh of heavily phased drums. On an album where at least half of the tracks would have made potential Top 10 singles, this was surely one of the strongest that never made it on to an A-side, although, three years later, it became the B-side to 'Don't Walk Away'.

5. 'Night in the City'

Another splendid tapestry of sound effects set the scene for a song evoking the feel of inner city claustrophobia, as two-note car horns morph into a recognisable rhythm and a powerful guitar riff. The lyrics evoke atmospheric pictures of travel, with a glimpse of freedom in a more relaxed setting far away—'standing at the airport looking down the street … standing at the dockside looking out to sea'. At one point, there is a collage of further motoring noises, culminating in what could be screeching brakes, keyboards, or screaming heavy metal guitar soloing—or it could possibly be a combination of all three. The music crossfades at the end with another almighty battery of similar sound effects, and altogether, it amounts to a wall of sound worthy of the style of Phil Spector at his most creative.

6. 'Starlight'

This could hardly be more of a contrast. Apparently inspired by the sound of soul singer Al Green, it opens with fairy dust synths, evoking memories of those big American orchestral numbers from the '30s and '40s into a relaxed four minutes of blue-eyed soul.

7. 'Jungle'

This is the album's most light-hearted moment, opening with bongos and a soundscape of animal noises, evoking the tropical rainforest. A short segment at the beginning of the bridge features the choir singing '*Im Dschungel, da tanzen die Tiere herum*' ('In the jungle, the animals are dancing around'). Some might regard it as a novelty song that has not worn too well, while to others, it is a rather charming number for children. The lyrics tell a Dr Dolittle-like story of a visitor coming to the jungle where a hundred animals have gathered under a pale moonlight, singing about a great blue ship that sails around the sun, and a friendly lion invites him to join them. It would take little imagination to see this as the basis for a children's cartoon or a picture book.

8. 'Believe Me Now'

About eighty seconds of lush orchestral instrumental with wordless vocals add up to a delightful breathing space, a curtain raiser for the next track.

9. 'Steppin' Out'

One of those songs that has grown in stature over the years, it was never a single, but it gradually became a favourite of fans, being the only track performed by Jeff Lynne's ELO at the Hyde Park concert in September 2014 that had never been a single; it also remained in the set list for the British dates of the tour, which began in April 2016. A short choral intro moves into a first verse with plaintive vocal and piano chords, on a song of sadness and hope, a theme of stepping out, and going to 'see the world'.

10-13 'Concerto for a Rainy Day'

A four-song suite taking up the whole of side three of the original album, this was based on the weather and its effects on mood change. The stormy weather effects heard on 'Concerto' were recorded by Lynne during an exceptionally wet few days in Munich during the summer of 1977 and used on the record. After three numbers, it ends with the promise of a brighter day in 'Mr Blue Sky'. For many, this was the centrepiece of the album, although a minority of critics remained resistant to its charm and grandeur. *All Music Guide* dismissed it as 'the nadir of the album, an effort at conceptual rock that seemed archaic even in 1977'—a view not widely shared.

10. 'Standin' in the Rain'

Used by the group as the opening on their *Out of the Blue* concerts, the first track opens the suite with haunting keyboard work over a recording of raindrops made outside the studio. About thirty seconds in there is a cymbal crash and clap of thunder, with the words 'Concerto for a Rainy Day' spoken by Tandy. One minute in, staccato strings are heard playing Morse code that spells out ELO. All this is the precursor to a blend of piano and lush strings, echoing vocal and synths, choral vocals, and a brief snatch of song with a couple of changes in tempo along the way.

11. 'Big Wheels'

Continuing with the theme of the weather and reflection, this begins with an introduction featuring a few seconds on classical-style piano, overlaid with vocoder, which would be heard a second time towards the end of 'Mr Blue Sky'. What follows is an ethereal, emotive ballad, suddenly building halfway through at the chorus with powerful strings and drums.

12. 'Summer and Lightning'

The wet-weather theme continues on this song, but with a progression to a more optimistic mood and lyrics. Another variation on the big ballad theme, it comes in the shape of an exuberant song with a breezy, summery melody. Acoustic guitar leads into impassioned vocals, developed with heavy strings, and about two-thirds of the way through it almost changes character completely with heavier percussion and oriental strings before the drama of the final chorus and fadeout, into yet more rain, segueing into 'Mr Blue Sky'.

13. 'Mr Blue Sky'

The album's second single, this reached No. 6 in Britain (ironically released in February 1978, shortly before parts of the country had their heaviest winter snowfall for several years) and a less spectacular No. 35 (Billboard) and No. 27 (Cashbox) in America. Although it was never their most successful single in terms of chart position or sales, it soon became and has always remained ELO's best-loved song, as well as the high point of the album. Written after several days of writer's block while staying in a Swiss chalet, Lynne stated: 'It was one of the first songs I ever wrote with really posh chords and a very simple melody, and I think it's the simplicity of the song and the tune. And the words are quite simple. It's like a nursery rhyme kind of thing, that's how I meant it to be'. He also then found that writing the remaining numbers on the album flowed easily.

A voice at the beginning announces quietly, 'Morning, please get us Mr Blue Sky'—compare calls of 'Full speed ahead!' before the last verse on The Beatles' 'Yellow Submarine'. Taking Fab Four references further, the piano chords are reminiscent of the middle section from The Beatles' 'A Day in the Life', on an extravaganza of effortlessly catchy feel-good tune, strings-soaked guitar solo, almost-out-of-breath vocals, and vocoder passage that comes to a sudden conclusion. It then starts again with a magnificent choral section and lush ending on the strings, repeating the phrase, as well as the subtly disguised instruction right at the end: 'Please turn me over', somewhat redundant when not heard at the end of side three on vinyl. All things considered, it adds up to what has been called 'five minutes of wistful, sentimental optimism which makes the listener feel for a short while that everything is right with the world'. As is so often the case with Lynne's productions of the time, it was enhanced by the chorus, orchestra, and additional touches, such as Bevan's little flourishes on cymbal.

The record has had a remarkably long shelf-life. After the official British charts also included weekly downloads from 2005 onwards, it re-entered the lower end of the Top 100 in 2011 and 2012 four times, most notably in August 2012 after being featured in the closing ceremony of the London Olympic Games. In February 2011, it was played at Wembley Stadium after the match in which Birmingham City Football Club won the League Cup Final, as well as at every home game, Lynne having been a lifelong staunch Blues fan. In 2014, it came first in a poll organised by youth charity Rhythmix to find Britain's favourite feel-good tune. Several others, including Joe Brown, Lily Allen, Rock Choir and the Delgados, have recorded it, as did Jim Bob (formerly of Carter the Unstoppable Sex Machine) as a theme tune to the BBC Radio 4 sitcom, also called *Mr Blue Sky*. It was also featured in several feature films and soundtracks—including *Eternal Sunshine of the Spotless Mind*, *The Game Plan*, *Role Models*, *Martin Child*, and *A Smile as Big as the Moon*—television programmes, such as *Doctor Who*, *CSI: Crime Scene Investigation*, and *American Dad!*, and in commercials for Volkswagen, Glidden House Paint, and Marks & Spencer.

When it was announced in the spring of 2016 that Jeff Lynne's ELO would play at the Glastonbury Festival that summer, *NME* wrote that nobody else among the line-up would have a song as iconic as this in their repertoire: 'Epic, comic, overwrought and wildly uplifting, it's the ultimate Glastonbury weather charm and your chance to pretend you're Dame Kiri Te Kanawa at the top of your voice for three minutes'.

14. 'Sweet is the Night'

One could hardly seek more of a contrast with the previous song than with this, one of the group's most impressive ballads, with melody, vocals, harmonies, guitar and strings all combining to form a song of extraordinary beauty. It boasts 'an embarrassment of epic choruses,' piled on 'with the enthusiasm of a Bake Off contestant piping rosettes on a showstopper … swept from an elegant glam-funk strut to a chorus that was essentially "All The Young Dudes" base-jumping'.[8] It also has what is surely the record's most eye-opening rhymes ever—'You start to sway, check your Cartier'.

15. 'The Whale'

The album's second instrumental is a more or less ambient and relatively simple piece with atmospheric keyboards. There are some spoken vocals on the vocoder, though it is difficult to make out exactly what is being said, although according to the Jeff Lynne Songs Database, it is probably 'here in the whole world the people will die'. As a rule, a piece like this might run the risk of sounding dull, but as an interlude in such a richly textured album, it comes as a well-placed breathing space—a moment of calm. A deeply moved Lynne wrote it after watching a documentary on the slaughter of whales, as did Jon Anderson who wrote the similarly themed 'Don't Kill the Whale', a single by Yes at around the same time. It appeared on the B-side of the American single 'It's Over', and all royalties were donated to a North Atlantic anti-whaling group. Some ten years later, part of the music was used as the sign-off each night on CFTO-TV, a Toronto television station.

16. 'Birmingham Blues'

A song about the group's home town is the closest the album comes to rock 'n' roll. There are a couple of snatches of acoustic rhythm guitar, more oriental strings that seem to be playing a snatch of Gershwin's 'Rhapsody in Blue', and a bluesy guitar riff. Although the theme of the lyrics is one of a local lad travelling the world and suffering the 'Birmingham blues' because he is missing his home city, the title was inspired partly by the local name for the Birmingham Blues local football team, the song thus being partly a tribute to them.

17. 'Wild West Hero'

The third single, and a British No. 6 hit (as were the second and fourth), conjures up childhood memories of watching westerns and dreaming of being the central figure in such fantasies. Lynne adds one of those remarkable little touches at the start—five seconds of tinkling, tinny bar room piano and clattering horse' hooves before switching instantly to the opening vocal line and strings. 'Wish I was a Wild West Hero,' he muses, in the first line of an introspective number about riding the desert sands, 'and into the prairie lands.' After the first bridge comes a wonderfully out-of-character moment led by a slow bluesy guitar riff and a snatch of honky-tonk piano again, played, unusually, not by Tandy but by Gale. On the second bridge is a breathtaking couple of lines sung a cappella, and the slow blues and strings (minus piano) take a bow again before the final chorus lines. In less skilled hands such an embarrassment of riches might have ended up as a total mess, but in Lynne's hands, the result was nothing short of remarkable.

'Wild West Hero' was almost a comparative flop. In its fourth week on the British charts in July 1978, it slid five places to No. 36. A speedy pressing of yellow vinyl 12" singles hitting the shops resulted in a swift jump to No. 24 and an eventual peak position of No. 6 during fourteen weeks on the Top 75, a feat unmatched by no other ELO single before or since.

Bonus Tracks

18. 'Wild West Hero'

A brief a cappella segment of the song suggesting work in progress, about twenty seconds using alternate lyrics that were not used on the finished version.

19. 'The Quick and the Daft'

An instrumental about 100 seconds long, alternating fast and slow passages, again sounding like the basis of an idea that would be incorporated into the other material.

20. 'Latitude 88 North'

This song was begun at around the same time, although it was only completed by Lynne around thirty years later. Tandy thought it sounded like a travel documentary with its references to 'frozen wastes and howling winds.' The strings are more restrained here than on the other songs on the album, and sound-wise, it has more in common with the folk-rock songs Lynne later recorded from the late 1980s onwards with George Harrison, Roy Orbison and with the Traveling Wilburys as a group. Like 'Surrender' from *A New World Record*, it was released as an iTunes digital download single to promote the reissued album in 2007, and was added to the Radio 2 playlist for a couple of weeks. About 300 copies were released as promotional one-sided 7" singles on transparent orange vinyl and quickly snapped up by collectors.

Discovery

UK:	Released May 1979, Jet/CBS, No. 1
US:	Released June 1979, Jet/Columbia, No. 4
Current edition:	Legacy/Sony CD

Personnel: Jeff Lynne: vocals, guitars, electric piano, Moog
Bev Bevan: drums, percussion
Richard Tandy: piano, clavinet, Moog, guitar, backing vocals
Kelly Groucutt: bass guitar, backing vocals
Louis Clark: orchestral and choral arrangements
Recorded at Musicland Studios, Munich, March–April 1979
Produced by Jeff Lynne

The group's first British No. 1 album entered the chart in June 1979 at peak position and stayed there for five weeks, a much better performance in Britain than America, as would be the case with subsequent releases. It was also the first in British chart history to generate four Top 10 singles or, strictly speaking, five—the last was a double A-side, a record broken three years later by Michael Jackson with 'Thriller'.

This record tends to divide fans sharply. To some it was a natural progression from the orchestral and progressive rock-meets-radio-friendly pop of the previous albums, adding dancefloor rhythms on a couple of tracks, especially given that *Out of the Blue* would be to ELO what *Hotel California* had been to The Eagles—a musical masterpiece that was hard to follow. To others it sounded slick and calculated, not to say superficial, even selling out to the disco crowd in the aftermath of the *Saturday Night Fever* soundtrack album having dominated British music the previous year. Playing around with the title (Disco Very, Very Disco) owned up to everything. Lynne admitted that he really liked 'that four-to-the-bar disco thing because [he] loved the strictness of it' and was keen to write more in that genre. He had already flirted with it in 'Doin' That Crazy Thing', a solo single in the summer of 1977 that sounded more like The Bee Gees than ELO, and received some Radio 1 exposure, but it never charted at home or overseas.

It also marked the start of a slimmed-down four-piece group. Kaminski, McDowell, and Gale were now no longer members; however they still appeared in the videos for every track, which were used to promote the album worldwide instead of another global tour. Lynne was increasingly disenchanted with playing live night after night, playing the same set on stage all the time, and made no secret of his preference for spending more time in the studios creating new music instead.

Tracks

1. 'Shine a Little Love'

Like the second, third, and fourth singles from the previous album, the first single from this album reached No. 6 in Britain; it begins, in what had become something of a tradition for the group, with a short passage lasting about thirty seconds. This has been identified as coming from a recording by a male voice choir of a German song, 'Die Blümelein sie schlafen' ('The flowers are long asleep'), with words by Anton Wilhelm Florentin von Zuccalmaglio and music by Johannes Brahms, published in 1858, sampled, distorted (with keyboard effects overlaid on top), slowed, and then reversed. This section was edited from the version released as a single and on compilation albums. From that there is a swift transition to the song's intro, showing at the same time something of a Philadelphia soul influence and a Bee Gees *Saturday Night Fever*-type vibe, clearly aimed at the discos, with cascading keyboard effects, handclaps, and call-and-respond vocals. In Lynne's own words, there was not only a disco beat 'and quite a lot of things going on', but it was also 'very jolly and bouncy and [he] must have been in a very good mood when [he] wrote it!' At the end of the vocal section, with the repetition of the phrase 'you shine a little love on my life and let me see', he can be heard calling out 'ELO' at one point. This was retained in concert performances during the 2016 tour.

For the benefit of collectors, this was released on 7" and 12" single, the latter in both black and white vinyl. Unusually, the black 12" is much the rarer pressing, and in November 2016, a copy auctioned on eBay reached a price of £190.85.

2. 'Confusion'

The track that became a double A-side with 'Last Train to London' was a wistful yet uplifting song (or according to *Face the Music* fanzine, 'an ABBA-esque bit of slush,' albeit with 'nice touches'). It features more of the cascading keyboard effects and is enlivened by the reggae-style rimshots and kettle drum fills. It was allegedly written while Lynne was playing snooker with footballer Trevor Francis, and was about to take his shot when he nipped into another room, jotted down the melody line in around three minutes, returned to the game and won.

3. 'Need Her Love'

A functional enough, not to say tender, but perhaps none-too-inspired love song. The guitar solo and piano chords combined with the strings bring the work of George Harrison to mind again. It was the first of three similar numbers on the record. Lynne was indeed in a romantic frame of mind during the making of this album. A few weeks after it was released, he and Sandi Kapelson were married.

4. 'The Diary of Horace Wimp'

The second British single, reaching No. 8, was the nearest the group ever came to a novelty song. The lyrics tell the story of a hapless 'nowhere man' who was urged to go out and find himself a wife; he gets married by the last verse and is then urged 'is this your wife, go out and find yourself a life'. Clever use is made of the vocoder, and as regards the rhythm, it carries on where 'Mr Blue Sky' left off.

5. 'Last Train to London'

Released as the fourth British single, a double A-side with 'Confusion' and a British No. 8 hit, it is the second disco-influenced song on the album, with its hints of 'Showdown'.

The dance-orientated bassline and infectious chorus make it one of his strongest disco-style numbers. To an extent, it is slightly autobiographical; Lynne later recalled that when writing it, he had in mind the time 'when it seemed [they] spent years on trains travelling back and forth between Birmingham and various TV and radio stations in London'. Atomic Kitten sampled the hook of the song in 'Be With You', a British No. 2 in 2002.

6. 'Midnight Blue'

This falls into the same category as 'Need Her Love', a pleasant enough, if rather syrupy or unremarkable love song. It was recorded by Carl Wayne on the various artists 2001 tribute album *Lynne Me Your Ears*.

7. 'On the Run'

An infectious pop number enhanced by a bubbling synthesiser hook. The intro was created with the use of a table tennis ball on a tennis table and a piece of glass from the studio where the drums were recorded. Lynne admitted that it seemed he was trying 'to make it the most annoying intro in the world, and it probably still is'. About a minute before the end, the tempo alters, slowing down at first and then speeding up.

8. 'Wishing'

The third of the album's love songs boasts an attractive tune, but it was weighed down by rather saccharine strings and lyrics. The reverse tape message just before the end—'I wish my wife was not away'—reveals his inspiration.

9. 'Don't Bring Me Down'

The third single was a British No. 3 and American No. 4, thus becoming their highest-charting single ever in either territory (and also No. 1 in Canada). Lynne made a last-minute decision at the end of the sessions to write and record this song as he realised there were not 'enough loud ones on the album'. It was in fact a solo recording, as well as the first ELO track released (if not recorded) without strings, built on a drum loop from 'On the Run', written on piano with guitars and bass added later. Lynne said that in addition to the drum loop, it included 'eight grand pianos, a cement mixer, and two crates of Newcastle Brown Ale and that got the ball rolling'. The word 'grooosss' in the chorus was made up on the spot because it fitted. Thinking it was actually 'Bruce', fans would sing it at live performances until Lynne eventually adopted it himself on stage. The sound heard at the end was a fire door at Musicland Studios being shut. This was apparently intended as a suitable ending as it was the last song on the album; it was as if to signify that the group had just finished work and were leaving the building.

The live version adds a more prominent guitar solo around two minutes in, while behind a couple of lines on the penultimate verse, piano and drums briefly switch the backing into rockabilly rhythm, and in the short bridge before the final verse, an inventive burst of piano comes to the fore.

In November 2007, Lynne was awarded a BMI Million-Air certificate in recognition of 2 million airplays for the record.

Bonus Tracks

10. 'On the Run'

A fragmentary sixty-second demo recorded by Lynne on his own in his home studio, with lyrics in a different order from the completed version.

11. 'Second Time Around'

Another fragment, lasting forty seconds, recorded by Lynne in his home studio. This ballad, backed with piano and vocal harmonies, was never completed.

12. 'Little Town Flirt' (Del Shannon and Maron McKenzie)

A rare example of an ELO cover version, this was begun at the *Discovery* sessions and completed by Lynne in 2001. It remains faithful to the arrangement of the original, which had been a British No. 4 and American No. 12 hit in 1963. Del Shannon had always been one of his heroes, as the first major act he ever saw live on stage during his teenage years. Coincidentally, Shannon was the first act other than ELO whom he produced, having worked with him and co-written songs with him during the mid-1970s, although only one was released at the time—'Cry Baby Cry', an American single in 1975. Lynne later co-wrote more songs with Shannon and helped to produce his final album *Rock On!*, which was released posthumously in 1991 about a year after he took his own life. As part of The Traveling Wilburys, he also recorded a new version of 'Runaway' as a tribute.

Xanadu

UK: Released August 1980, Jet/CBS, No. 2
US: Released August 1980, MCA, No. 4 (Billboard), No. 1 (Cashbox)
Current edition: Legacy/Sony CD
Recorded at Musicland Studios, 1979–80
Personnel as *Discovery*, plus vocals by Olivia Newton-John (title track, plus non-ELO tracks only)
Produced by Jeff Lynne (ELO tracks only)

Although not an official ELO album, the group were responsible for five of the ten tracks, the others featuring Olivia Newton-John as well as singing with Gene Kelly, Cliff Richard, and The

Tubes. It is the soundtrack of a movie starring Newton-John, who was then hot property in the wake of her success co-starring and singing with John Travolta in *Grease*, and who also appeared with ELO on the title song. As an album, the record was a success, reaching No. 2 in Britain (US Billboard No. 4, Cashbox No. 1), although the movie came to be regarded as a box office disaster. ELO's credibility took something of a knock because of their association with a project appealing more to the pop than the rock market, with Bevan later admitting that *Xanadu* 'wasn't really [them]'. The group never performed any of the songs live during their remaining six years together, though ELO Part II sometimes featured the title song with Groucutt on lead vocal.

Tracks

1. 'I'm Alive'

The first single, reaching No. 20, begins with one of Tandy's ambient synth introductions, which is overtaken by a thunderous assault of bass and drums, with call-and-respond vocals, and a strong hook on the chorus. About two-thirds of the way through comes a temporary change in pace, with a near-explosion of phased drums and keyboards followed by a swift reprise of the chorus.

2. 'The Fall'

The only track not released as a single in Britain starts with a heartbeat-like bassline and a vocal, which sounds like it was recorded down a telephone. After a few seconds, drums come in and it reverts to more normal song-mode, with a balance between ethereal-sounding verses and a punchier chorus.

3. 'Don't Walk Away'

A No. 21 hit in Britain, and a straightforward, yet haunting love and heartbreak song, on which the backing builds effectively from simple piano and synths to a crescendo towards the fade. This is generally considered superior to the ballads on *Discovery*.

4. 'All Over the World'

The second single and a No. 11 hit in Britain opens to the sound of overdubbed party noises, then becoming a semi-disco tempo number similar to 'Evil Woman'. The lyrics include a sly reference to Shard End, Lynne's birthplace in Birmingham, in the same line as other cities of the world, such as New York, London, Paris, and Rome. As the group were now undertaking much less live work between 1980 and 1986, this song was never played on stage until Lynne returned with Jeff Lynne's ELO at the Hyde Park concert of September 2014, when he chose it as the opening number. By then, it had achieved greater status as the title track of the very successful 2005 compilation album.

5. 'Xanadu'

For the first and last time, ELO had a British No. 1 single, albeit shared billing with the woman who could do no wrong chart-wise at the time. In America, it reached No 8. With a glittering fairy dust-style intro, it features backing vocals from Lynne and probably Groucutt. In common with many 'star collaborations' recorded at around the time, Newton-John added her contribution to the backing track in a different studio with none of the group present. Lynne recorded a more stripped-down version in 2000 in Traveling Wilburys-style with minor lyrical changes, credited to ELO but a one-man effort apart from Marc Mann on keyboards; it was released on the 2010 compilation *Flashback*. Several other artists, including Sharleen Spiteri of Texas and Dannii Minogue, have also recorded the song.

Time

UK:	Released July 1981, Jet/CBS, No. 1
US:	Released August 1981, Jet/Columbia, No. 16
Current edition:	Legacy/Sony CD
Personnel:	Jeff Lynne: vocals, guitars, keyboards
	Bev Bevan: drums, percussion
	Richard Tandy: keyboards, guitars
	Kelly Groucutt: bass guitar, backing vocals
	Rainer Pietsch: strings

Recorded at Musicland Studios, Munich, and Polar Studios, Stockholm, 1981
Produced by Jeff Lynne

Topping the album charts for two weeks, this was the first album credited to the group by their initials, although DJs and the press had done so for years by this time. In the early 1980s, the synth-pop of the Human League, Ultravox, and others was the dominant force in British music, a climate in which the increasingly keyboard-orientated ELO were very much at home, and much of the drumming sounds like it was programmed. Like *Eldorado* it is a concept album, based in this instance on the story of a man from the 1980s who time-travels to the year 2095, where he is torn between a fascination with technological advancement and a longing to return to the earlier age. Some regarded it as a return to form after the ultra-commercial *Discovery*, while others thought it too computerised and lacking in warmth.

Although they were now a quartet in the studios, they expanded to a seven-piece when touring the record over 1981–82, with Louis Clark on keyboards, plus Kaminski and long-time Birmingham friend and associate Dave Morgan on rhythm guitar and backing vocal. Clark had been temporarily replaced as strings arranger by Rainer Pietsch as he had commitments elsewhere associated with the success of his *Hooked on Classics* work at the time of recording. The 2001 reissue added three bonus tracks recorded at the sessions, two issued as B-sides and one on *Afterglow*.

Tracks

1. 'Prologue/Twilight'

The 'Prologue' starts with backward running synths as a vocoder monologue talks about 'Just on the border of your waking mind', segueing into 'Twilight' itself in a massive explosion of phased drumming and an ultra-catchy bubbling keyboard hook. Two-thirds of the way through, a short bridge slows down the pace before another explosion in one of Lynne's most dazzlingly inventive tracks from the post-strings era. Another backwards secret message comes at the end, with 'Though you ride on the wheels of tomorrow, You still wander the fields of your sorrow' played in reverse.

When released as a single, reaching No. 30 in Britain, it had an unenthusiastic reception on BBC Radio 1's weekly new singles review programme *Round Table*. By then, the station's cheerleader for alternative and indie music, John Peel, dismissed it as 'rock music for Social Democrats' (the recently formed Social Democratic Party were riding high in national opinion polls at the time, with Conservative and Labour supporters—Peel being a staunch socialist—correctly predicting it would not last).

2. 'Yours Truly, 2095'

A song about genuine romance in the microchip era—in Lynne's words, about a man who falls in love with a robot. With a keyboard hook and distorted vocals reminiscent of The Buggles' 1979 chart-topper 'Video Killed The Radio Star' and a few seconds from a pinball machine in the studio in Germany, it evokes a futuristic world with clever allusions to someone or something, using the words 'does the things you do, but she is an IBM' and 'her memory banks overflow'. Lynne's wife, Sandi, makes a brief uncredited appearance as the robot speaking the final chorus as Tandy's keyboards bring the song to a dramatic conclusion.

3. 'Ticket to the Moon'

The third single, reaching No. 23, shifts the subject matter from time travel to space travel and romance, in a ballad that includes moon landing sound effects as well as a tinkling piano and synths. Lynne sings of having a ticket to faraway places: 'But I'd rather see the sunrise in your eyes'.

4. 'The Way Life's Meant to Be'

This, the fourth single and the only ELO release between 1977 and 1986, which fell completely short of the British charts, begins with what sounds like a few seconds of keyboard-mimicking strings and acoustic rhythm guitar. A slightly Spanish rhythm is emphasised by castanets. Lyrically, it is a doomy futuristic tale of the time traveller wandering around 'this wreck of a town ... with its ivory towers and its plastic flowers', while musically, the melody line bears some similarity to that of 'Across the Border' from *Out of the Blue*. It also has what is a rarity on this album: a guitar solo—a twangy affair reminiscent of Duane Eddy, one of the acts with whom he would go on to work as writer, musician, and producer later in the decade. Bevan said that a '60s feel was intentional, and that they had a Phil Spector-type production and arrangement in mind while it was being recorded.

5. 'Another Heart Breaks'

An instrumental, this is Lynne's effort to make an Oberheim synthesiser sound like a guitar. Pretty sounding, if rather unadventurous and unashamedly influenced by The Shadows, it hovers between two phrases of two chords each.

6. 'Rain is Falling'

Some saw this ballad as an answer song to 'Mr Blue Sky' or at least a continuation of 'Concerto for a Rainy Day' (inevitably). In Lynne's words, it was simply 'about some scientists trying to mess with time', with doomy lyrics about bad weather, thunder, and lightning.

7. 'From the End of the World'

Ushered in by a few seconds of backward-running strings, this introduction to a song with a whirring keyboard is rather reminiscent in a way to some of Joe Meek's early 1960s work (notably the Tornados' 'Telstar'—with the similarity becoming more marked towards the end) and electronic backbeat, plus a swift crescendo on drums to finish.

8. 'The Lights Go Down'

Moving close to reggae territory, this one lyrically has a mood of sadness, in which 'things are going wrong, and the night goes on and on'.

9. 'Here is the News'

Less a song than a sound collage and another Buggles' sound-alike, this is made up of tinkling synths, including electronic pips, voices subjected to vocoder trickery, and voices made to sound like radio news broadcasts. Some stations contacted the group later to claim that they had used pieces of their broadcasts without authorisation, to which Lynne replied that they had all been constructed by him in the studio.

10. '21st Century Man'

Said to be a tribute to John Lennon, who had been killed the previous year, this is an acoustic ballad about a man who rides 'on the wheels of tomorrow' and will 'wander the fields of your sorrow', echoing the backwards message on 'Twilight'. The verses might recall the tune of Ralph McTell's 'Streets of London' to mind in places.

11. 'Hold On Tight'

The album's first single, reaching No. 4 in Britain and No. 10 in America, comes as light relief after the rather downbeat nature of much of the record. It was intentional as Lynne admitted that several of the preceding songs were 'getting a bit doomy'; it is a snappy, infectious piece of rockabilly with buzzsaw guitar, boogie-woogie piano, and optimistic lyrics. The French lyrics in the third verse were translated from English by the French nanny at the Lynnes' home in France, where his wife and small daughters were staying.

12. 'Epilogue'

A ninety-second closer to the original album reprises the 'wheels of tomorrow' and 'fields of your sorrow' couplet, and the spoken phrase 'Let me rise from this day forward, in a world of time' (though the latter part is somewhat obscured and open to doubt), with a few backward sound effects at the end, perhaps indicative of the time-traveller's return.

Bonus Tracks

13. 'The Bouncer'

The B-side of 'Four Little Diamonds' (see p. 64), this upbeat track with a comparatively rocky guitar introduction changes rhythm for the last minute or so to a rolling blues. The word 'bouncer' is not mentioned in the lyrics, and it is a straightforward love song with the narrator looking forward to his loved one returning home.

Thereby hangs a mystery: 'The Bouncer' was originally announced in the music press as an instrumental recorded during the sessions for *Time*, which was to be a non-album B-side for 'Hold on Tight'. Lynne wrote in the sleeve notes for the 2001 remaster of *Time* that it was recorded late in the album sessions as he 'needed a loud one', and that the background vocals were inspired by Monty Python's Mounties Choir. ELO experts think it more likely that the song, clearly not an instrumental, was recorded during the 'Secret Messages' sessions. As the title does not appear in the lyrics, there is a theory that it was given the wrong title in error, and that the vaults still contain an instrumental named 'Bouncer'.

14. 'When Time Stood Still'

The B-side of 'Hold on Tight' is dominated by tinkling synths and piano, in keeping with the electronic feel of much of the album, in contrast to the other two bonus tracks. The lyrics paint a bleak portrait in words of a lonely man in a lonely world, where there are no pictures on an empty wall, and just echoes in ivory halls when time stood still.

15. 'Julie Don't Live Here'

The B-side of 'Twilight' is a very commercial tune, 'a little pop song about a girl next door who is now in another dimension' according to its writer that has an intro with shades of The Crystals' 'Then He Kissed Me' and even a touch of Beach Boys-like harmonies.

Secret Messages

UK:	Released June 1983, Jet/CBS, No 4
US:	Released June 1983, Jet/Columbia, No 36
Current edition:	Legacy/Sony CD
Personnel:	Jeff Lynne: vocals, guitars, bass guitar, keyboards
	Bev Bevan: drums, percussion
	Richard Tandy: keyboards, guitars
	Kelly Groucutt: bass guitar, backing vocals (tracks 10, 11, 12)
	Mik Kaminski: violin (track 11)
	Louis Clark: strings (tracks 7, 8, 10)

Recorded at Wisseloord Studios, Hilversum, December 1982–February 1983
Produced by Jeff Lynne

This album had a difficult history. It was planned and first announced to the press as an eighteen-track double with a working title of *Unexpected Moments*, the original concept being the package of a single disc of new material and—despite Lynne's lack of enthusiasm for live albums—one live disc, either made up of recordings from the *Time* tour or of the 1978 Wembley concert. A double album would have completed Lynne's contract and left him free to disband ELO at any time afterwards. However, he was never a fan of live albums and soon he had written and recorded enough new songs for two discs of fresh material. A track listing was drawn up and acetates were produced, and only then did Jet Records' distributor CBS request its reduction to a single album. It was ironic in view of the fact that in 1983 some artists were starting to release albums on vinyl and CD simultaneously, and the full seventy-minute set could have fitted on the new format, instead of being curtailed to two sides of a 12" vinyl album with a playing time of around forty minutes. All but one of the tracks thus rejected appeared as B-sides on subsequent singles and on the three-CD compilation *Afterglow* boxed set in 1990 (see p. 91). Rumours that the complete album would be released one day have yet to materialise, although every track, except for the legendary 'Beatles Forever', has been legitimately issued in one form or another.

Kaminski returned to play on one track, Clark returned to conduct strings on three others, and Groucutt likewise appeared on only three. Later that year, he left the group and began legal action for unpaid royalties, being awarded a settlement out of court. The group were no longer touring, and with Lynne programming most of the drums, an increasingly frustrated Bevan, who found himself required for little more than hitting the cymbals at the right places, was now also working with Black Sabbath, leading to rumours that he had left ELO to join them indefinitely.

The original track listing:

Side 1: 'Secret Messages*/Loser Gone Wild*/Bluebird*/Take Me On and On'*

Side 2: 'Stranger*/No Way Out***/Beatles Forever§/Letter from Spain*/Danger Ahead'*

Side 3: 'Four Little Diamonds*/Train of Gold*/Endless Lies*****/Buildings Have Eyes****/Rock 'n' Roll is King'*

Side 4: 'Mandalay****/Time After Time**/After All***/Hello My Old Friend'****

*	on 1983 LP
**	on 1983 LP, cassette and CD
***	bonus tracks on 2001 CD reissue
****	only on *Afterglow*
*****	only on *Afterglow*, alternate version on *Balance of Power*
§	still unreleased

It only exists in this form on a few acetate pressings. Lynne has blocked official release, and it seems unlikely that he will change his mind. One of these acetates was sold by auction on eBay in December 2005 for $6,850, about £4,000 sterling.

'Beatles Forever'—with lyrics drawn mainly from Lennon-McCartney titles, brief musical quotes from 'Please Please Me' and 'From Me to You', and refrain of 'Beatles forever, Rolling Stones never'—remains unofficially unreleased. According to Groucutt in an interview shortly before the album's release, it was 'one of those songs that you know is going to be a smash while you're working on it', and he confidently predicted that it would be a big hit single. Why it was shelved—and unlike the other tracks not released at the time, it has never appeared on a B-side or on any subsequent compilation—has been the subject of much speculation. It has been suggested that there might have been copyright issues in its heavy reliance on titles, though this could surely have been circumvented. The lack of reference to any Harrison numbers (the opening line 'there's something about a Beatles song' apart) might have been embarrassing in view of their later working relationship, and likewise dismissive comments on the Rolling Stones. Alternatively, Lynne may have thought it below his usual standard and talked of rewriting what he called his 'fawning' lyrics, which sound a little twee, or even starting again from scratch.

The song was once played at an ELO Fan Club Convention, at which a poor-quality bootleg recording was secretly made and later uploaded to YouTube. Lynne recycled the chorus in 'Video!', one of two tracks he contributed to the soundtrack of the movie *Electric Dreams* in 1984, both of which included Tandy on keyboards.

Tracks

1. 'Secret Messages'

This begins with a few seconds of electronica, the title being whispered amid a whirl of Morse code and associated sounds before the bubbling synthesisers and guitar work take over in another helping of Buggles-like pop. The song was released as the album's second British single, but despite the boost of a 7" picture disc linked to a competition, it stalled at No. 48 in Britain.

2. 'Loser Gone Wild'

At over five minutes, the album's longest track begins as a slow, melodramatic song with much echo on the vocals and a moody trumpet-like sound on the synthesiser, giving way to a reggae-fied chorus. The use of different time signatures is effective, and a jazzy guitar solo follows the second chorus.

3. 'Bluebird'

One of the strongest tunes here, with acoustic guitar prominent in the backing at first, interrupted by a couple of slow passages that seem about to take the song in a different direction before it reverts to the initial tune.

4. 'Take Me On and On'

Very like the kind of semi-ambient pop that became so pervasive in the British mid-1980s music scene, but rather short on tune. As Lynne said in the notes to the 2001 CD reissue, he was writing most of the songs on an Oberheim keyboard by now. Delicate synthesisers, a minimum of guitar soloing, and programmed drum effects weave their way around a lazy song, inspired by watching a TV documentary on the Space Shuttle, with lyrics describing the thoughts of how it would be to fly in space to the accompaniment of suitably timeless, drifting music.

5. 'Time After Time'

Released on the cassette and CD formats but not on the LP, this returns to the theme of 'Kuiama' ten years earlier in commenting on the futility of war, with Lynne's then wife, Sandi, on backing vocals. About three minutes of machine-like synth-pop ends in an explosion and the gentle sound of a childlike piano until the fade.

6. 'Four Little Diamonds'

A welcome return to rock 'n' roll, or very close to it, possibly reflecting the influence of Dave Edmunds, whom Lynne had recently produced. There is a feel of urgency in the lead and rhythm guitars and an attractively dated (in the best possible way) organ, while the lyrics tell the story of a man who gives his intended a diamond ring and never sees her again. As the third British single, it could only manage an underwhelming peak of No. 84 in Britain (No. 86 in America).

7. 'Stranger'

Starting with a backwards message saying, 'You're playing me backwards' (obvious, perhaps), this flows gently with some pleasant keyboards and gentle lead guitar, although it sounds like one of those sings that longs to burst into a build-up near the end and never quite does.

8. 'Danger Ahead'

Another welcome more upbeat number. Lynne had recently produced some tracks for Dave Edmunds and the tune of this song, plus some upfront guitar, faintly Beach Boys-like backing vocals, adventurous strings from Clark, and, at last, some forceful drumming—Bevan being allowed more or less free rein on this occasion—instead of programming, make this one of the standout tracks.

9. 'Letter from Spain'

A solo track featuring all vocals and instruments by Lynne, this was another reversion to ambient seasonal sounds, reminiscent of much of Brian Wilson's early 1970s output with The Beach Boys and of The Style Council's 'Long Hot Summer', a major hit in the summer of 1983. It starts softly and continues in that vein throughout, but fails to go anywhere. Lynne said it was going to be 'Letter from France', but 'Spain' might be sailing less close to the wind. It was later used in the international campaign to promote the 1992 Barcelona Olympic Games.

10. 'Train of Gold'

This sounds like a more laid-back cousin of 'Showdown'. Soul strings, oriental effects, and echoing vocals, all topped off by an effortless, but effective guitar solo, and something of a nod to Sherbet's 1976 hit 'Howzat'.

11. 'Rock 'n' Roll is King'

The only major hit single, No. 15 in Britain and No. 19 in America, closed the original album. Although seen as a rather lightweight affair with clichéd lyrics, its rockabilly swing and boogie piano, plus the return of Kaminski's fiddle on the lead break, ensures the album ends on a lively note. There is an echo of ELO's major hit from ten years earlier in that 'she rolled over Beethoven and she gave Tchaikovsky back'. In keeping with the album's title, it is prefaced on the spacey-sounding five-second snippet with the words 'Thank you for listening'—reversed, naturally. At the end is another ambient aural bookend, lasting about twenty-five seconds, over which a voice twice intones the words 'Welcome to the show'. The joke, naturally, was that this came at the end of the record, rather than the beginning. Some people just love being contrary.

Bevan said in a radio interview at the time that it was the record company's decision to put it out as the single, probably as it was in the same vein as 'Hold On Tight' from the previous album: 'We didn't care what they released, really, to be honest.... It doesn't particularly fit in with the rest of the stuff'.

Bonus Tracks

12. 'No Way Out'

In an unexpected departure from the norm, the relaxed, finger-clicking jazzy feel and rippling cocktail make this sound more like a Harold Arlen song from the interwar period than ELO. After a false fade, it returns with a short 'Strawberry Fields Forever' stop-start again type ending.

13. 'Endless Lies'

This ballad sounds almost like two songs fused together. A verse with its references to a merry-go-round and hints of a fairground steam organ gives way suddenly to a more urgent drumming sound and a chorus, suggesting homage to Lynne's hero Orbison, in some of whose last recordings he would shortly have a major hand. Lynne said he tried to sing it 'big' in the style of his hero: 'Obviously not as "big" as him, but I just tried to get that tone of voice. I played it to Roy Orbison as well and he liked it. It was just really a bit of fantasy singing with a bigger voice. I nearly succeeded'. An alternate version, almost thirty seconds shorter, subsequently appeared on *Balance of Power*.

14. 'After All'

This slow guitar and keyboard instrumental was originally intended not as a standalone track, but as a forty-second introduction to the eight-minute 'Hello My Old Friend'. It was extended to over two minutes and released on the B-side of 'Rock 'n' Roll is King'; Lynne reworked the idea for 'Night Calls', a song he wrote and produced as the title track of Joe Cocker's album of the same name in 1992.

Balance of Power

UK:	Released March 1986, Epic, No 9
US:	Released February 1986, Columbia, No 49
Current edition:	Legacy/Sony CD

Personnel: Jeff Lynne: vocals, guitars, bass guitar, keyboards, percussion
Bev Bevan: drums, percussion
Richard Tandy: keyboards, guitars
Christian Schneider: saxophone

Recorded at Compass Point Studios, Nassau, and Hartmann Digital Studios, Untertrubach, mixed at Musicland Studios, Munich, December 1984–February 1986
Produced by Jeff Lynne

Now more a contractual obligation than anything else—all ties having been severed with former manager Don Arden and the Jet label—Lynne, Bevan, and Tandy completed their joint partnership as ELO with an album completely free of strings. Lynne and Tandy were relying more heavily on synthesisers and electronic percussion, with Bevan's drumming hardly in evidence, and the addition of a saxophonist on two tracks. In contrast to the previous outer sleeves, often conveying a feeling of other-worldliness with their intricate designs, this time it was reduced to an austere, not to say soulless, geometrically shaped logo on a solid red background. It peaked in its second week of release in Britain at No. 9. At just over thirty-four minutes' running time, it was the shortest album they had yet released.

Four additional numbers that were recorded at the same sessions, 'Destination Unknown', 'Caught in a Trap', 'Matter of Fact', and 'Sorrow About to Fall', were omitted from the running order and appeared on the B-sides of or as bonus tracks on 7" and 12" singles.

Superficially, it may sound for the most part like an upbeat pop album, but a closer listen to the lyrics suggests otherwise. Perhaps Lynne was hinting at sadness at the imminent last chapter of ELO, the end of an era with putting the band to rest after fifteen years, albeit a band from which he had long wished to move on. On a more personal level, it coincided with the end of his second marriage. The album might therefore have been another with strong themes of breakup, alongside Bob Dylan's *Blood on the Tracks*, Phil Collins's *Face Values*, and Richard Thompson's *Hand of Kindness*. Lynne denied at the time that the album was in any way a personal one, insisting that it was 'all fictional stuff', but it comes across as a far more personal album than anything else by ELO. He said that all lyrics were written in the studios, half in Nassau and half in Germany, that their immediate surroundings played a part in the lyrical moods, and that they were the most instant sets of words he had ever done. As for the subject matter, he admitted that some songs were about relationships, but declined to elaborate further. A clue came almost thirty years later, in 2014, when he was presented with an award for Outstanding Contribution to Music at the Classic Rock Honours in Los Angeles. In his acceptance speech, he mentioned that many of his old songs had evolved in some way or other, taking on new meanings over the years. Some that he had thought were very straightforward were not after all: 'I sing them now and I realise what they're about and it's usually about grim stuff like relationships and crap relationships'.[9]

Tracks

1. 'Heaven Only Knows'

The opening track gets the album off to a lively start, with a catchy keyboard hook and infectious tune, shot through with strong vocal harmonies and a powerful guitar solo after the second chorus. It is all rather at odds with the chorus and theme of 'walking down a straight and lonely road'.

2. 'So Serious'

The album's second British single, reaching No. 77, is another deceptively upbeat number failing to conceal a sad theme, with the narrator lying awake night after night as he tries to fit it all together. It is a song of going separate ways: '[Being] so serious, to be all broken up and delirious, I guess we've really been out of touch'. The group promoted it on the BBC TV show *Wogan* (with Kenneth Williams standing in), miming with Mik Kaminski on violin, alongside Louis Clark and Dave Morgan on cellos, although none of these instruments had been used on the track or the album. Various aspects of the song have common ground with 'S.O.S.', and other tracks written and produced by Lynne (as well as including the playing of Lynne and Richard Tandy) on Dave Edmunds' 1984 album *Riff Raff*.

3. 'Getting to the Point'

The third British single and a disappointing No. 97, partly as result of industrial action at the CBS pressing plant, made a rather lame conclusion to what had generally been a good ten-year run of hits. Musically, it is a big production ballad that eschews an intro, another song of sadness about a situation 'out of control'. The keyboards produce a good impression of strings, culminating in a saxophone solo, which turns it in to rather generic Anglo-American middle-of-the-road mid-1980s pop that was in fashion at the time but now sounds oddly dated.

4. 'Secret Lives'

Another song that proves to be more than it appears at first listen features a bouncy keyboard hook and yet another sublimely infectious chorus despite being a slightly uncomfortable number, lyrically at least. It is addressed to somebody, alternatively in the second person and sometimes mentioned in the third person ('you' and 'she'), as the narrator wishes he knows what is wrong, and he wonders where she goes to in the night in her 'secret lives'. For the most part, the backing is synthesiser and drum programming, while it builds up on the chorus where real drums (presumably) enter at last, with a touch of twangy lead guitar, something which happens too rarely on this record.

5. 'Is it Alright'

As the title suggests, this is another song of sadness. On the surface, it is another hook-laden three minutes of sprightly synth-pop-dance that would not have sounded out of place on a Depeche Mode album. Then a listen to the lyrics reveals a letter to Jo. The narrator does not know where to begin so he says hello and asks her if it is now better that she is on her own, she is back where she belonged, and that she has what she wants.

6. 'Sorrow About to Fall'

This number does not alter the general downbeat mood either. Lyrically, the mood is not one about personal relationships breaking down, but a rather more eerie feeling of doom and gloom, even of imminent apocalypse. The title might suggest the aftermath of a love affair and a broken heart, but the theme goes deeper than that. In fact, there is silence in the city, nobody is about as everyone has moved to higher ground, and, most ominous of all, something has happened to the seasons. Musically, it is one of those that can trace its ancestry back to 'Showdown', an electropop tune with Schneider's saxophone supplying lines between the vocals and a vaguely 'Superstition'-like keyboard gently bubbling away. Had it been recorded a few years earlier, say at the time of *Out of the Blue*, one could imagine a few doom-laden sound effects or even the odd explosion to enhance the mood.

7. 'Without Someone'

This track was a return to the more ambient, dreamy numbers; pleasant, but unexceptional, with soft synthesisers, very restrained drum programming, and massive echo on the chorus vocals. The keyboards and guitar build up briefly during a break before the final choruses.

8. 'Calling America'

The first and most successful single from the album; this reached No. 28 in Britain and No. 18 in America, where it was to be their final chart entry. Returning to a theme Lynne first explored in 'Telephone Line', it told the story of someone 'out in space, trying to talk to someone', only to find that there was nobody on the other end—'there must be something going wrong, that number just rings on and on'. An infectious mid-tempo tune can hardly conceal the mood of frustration or even despair in the lyrics. During the group's final live dates in England and Germany in 1986, this was the only track featured from *Balance of Power*, thus underlining Lynne's evident lack of interest in promoting it.

9. 'Endless Lies'

A slightly shorter, recorded or perhaps remixed version of the ballad from the *Secret Messages* sessions (see above).

10. 'Send It'

This ends the album on a more upbeat note, following the tradition of previous albums in finishing with a rock 'n' roll tune. This time it is a straightforward twelve-bar blues—working with Dave Edmunds had evidently left its mark. Lynne called it 'a rockabilly record with brushes and synthesisers', triggered off by Bevan's wire brushes on the drums, plus guitar well down in the mix and thus barely audible.

Bonus Tracks

11. 'Opening/Heaven Only Knows'

This consists of a twenty-second prologue, an atmospherically enhanced single chord segueing into a slightly different version of the song. Instead of the infectious keyboard hook, there is a short verse, maybe more in keeping with the title, as Lynne prefaces it with a short verse beginning, 'Our Father, who art in heaven, I don't understand'. It would have made a more powerful, if less catchy, first track in the tradition of previous albums. On the other hand, the general impression is that the new three-piece synth-pop act were reinventing themselves for the final chapter as a contemporary mid-1980s outfit, maintaining little connection with their roots. Or perhaps, as other bonus tracks suggest, Lynne had deliberately omitted the more lyrically controversial material in favour of more anodyne, less pointed songs about the age-old themes of love and loss. By the time these were released for public consumption over twenty years later, enough water had passed under the bridge for any targets of his frustration or anger not to take any offence.

12. 'In for the Kill'

Previously unreleased in any form, first impressions are of an undistinguished synth-pop tune and introductory two-chord riff bubbling away in and out of the vocals much of the time. It is in fact an earlier version of 'Caught in a Trap' (see below). One of Lynne's angriest lyrics—'Doesn't matter who they are/Doesn't matter where/Some people can't get enough/That is their only care'—is on a par with Roger Waters' 'Have a Cigar' from Pink Floyd's *Wish You Were Here*, a no-punches-pulled commentary on music business greed. In the first two verses, Lynne gives the men in suits (managers or former managers and accountants, one assumes) both barrels with images of listening to the money talking, being in it for the thrill of the power game, and, most telling of all, people sitting in a darkened room while somebody holds out a document and smiles as hands are shaken all round.

13. 'Secret Lives'

An alternate take, about five seconds shorter than the released version with slightly heavier percussion.

14. 'Sorrow About to Fall'

Another alternate mix, similar to the original but almost twenty seconds shorter.

15. 'Caught in a Trap'

Son of 'In for the Kill', dominated by the same repetitive rhythm on keyboards and programmed drums. With their theme of being 'caught in a dead end', allusions to people who never learn, but 'keep on stalling', and the admission (or warning) that 'you gotta move with the times', the lyrics and title were presumably a comment on his situation in longing to be free of the group.

16. 'Destination Unknown'

Relegated on initial release to side two of the 12" single of 'Calling America', this is surely the strongest track from the final sessions, and its inclusion on the album would have enhanced it considerably. The verses are based around three chords, almost a twelve-bar blues, until the bridge. In contrast to most of the other songs, it is part-pulsating pop-rock tune, with prominent saxophone on the introduction as well as on the break, part reggae (particularly in the bridge), and, at last, what sounds like the solid attack of genuine drums. At one moment, it is a little like M's 'Pop Muzik', at other times, it is reminiscent of Status Quo during their more commercial 1980s phase—or even Wizzard.

Any listener will realise that the lyrics have nothing to do with space travel or exploration. With a message of 'getting out of here', 'had enough of the confusion' (an allusion to one of their greatest hits, possibly), and being 'tired of playing other people's games', it might have been Lynne's final goodbye and good riddance to ELO (increasingly just a contractual obligation) and a 'hello' to the excitement of an uncertain but promising career outside the comfort zone, primarily on further productions for others. In this case, it would have been even more appropriate as the last track on *Balance of Power*, something that would happen in 2007 with the release of the remastered CD containing all six bonus tracks.

Zoom

UK:	Released June 2001, Epic, No. 34
US:	Released June 2001, Columbia, No. 94
Current edition:	Frontiers
Personnel:	Jeff Lynne: lead and backing vocals, guitars, bass guitar, piano, keyboards, cello, drums Richard Tandy: piano (track 1) Suzie Katayama: cello (tracks 4, 5, 12) Marc Mann: guitar (track 2),

string arrangements (tracks 6, 11)
Rosie Vela: backing vocals (tracks 1, 12), dance (tap), string arrangements
Dave Boruff: saxophone (track 10)
Roger Lebow: cello (track 13)
George Harrison: slide guitar (tracks 10, 12)
Ringo Starr: drums (tracks 2, 7)
Kris Wilkinson: string arrangements (track 9)

Recorded at Jeff Lynne's Home Studio, Los Angeles, 1998–2001
Produced by Jeff Lynne

The first new album released under the group name for fifteen years entered the British album chart at No. 34, and in America reached No. 94. Having reclaimed full rights to the name Electric Light Orchestra in 1999, after several years of producing for others and making a solo album, Lynne recorded eighteen newly written and recorded songs—fourteen of which, including one on the Japanese edition only, have been released—on which he contributed most of the vocals and instruments. Only one previous member, Richard Tandy, who had declined an invitation to take part in ELO Part II, took part. Two former Beatles—George Harrison, in one of the last recordings he made before his death in November 2001, and Ringo Starr—also participated in the sessions. The other musicians included Suzie Katayama, who had played cello on one of Jeff's productions for Starr nine years earlier; Rosie Vela, who had enjoyed brief success in Britain in the mid-1980s, on backing vocals; and Lynne's daughter, Laura, also on backing vocals.

In an interview shortly after its release, Lynne said that, since disbanding the group, he had broadened his musical experience, and that working with the other four members of the Traveling Wilburys had influenced how he sculpted the ELO sound on *Zoom*. He had learned much from working with others, and believed that it opened him up more while he was locked away at home, working on fresh material. It was recorded over two and a half years at his Los Angeles home recording studio and in various rooms throughout the house, utilising built-in dramatic acoustics. The songs themselves, he commented, drew on life's ups and downs, some quite personal in their own way, with the words and ideas in general coming to him much faster than they used to in earlier days as he was basing them more on things that had happened to him. He stressed that his new lyrics were 'more heartfelt' than previously: '[Some were] about just trying to do as good as you can when things don't work out. Sometimes there are loose ends that you can never tidy up. But it's also about trying to learn to trust your instincts and do what you feel is right'.[10]

Being released at a time when Lynne had had a low profile as a performer for some years, it received little publicity and was largely ignored except by the faithful. In retrospect, it is seen, if not exactly as a classic, certainly as an enjoyable work that was superior to at least the last two ELO albums in suggesting that Lynne's muse was reinvigorated; it definitely deserved a wider audience than it received on its muted reception.

Tracks

1. 'Alright'

This rock 'n' rolling blues number is an optimistic song of contentment. A blistering fuzz-tone guitar solo enlivens matters further about halfway through, as do a couple of brief variations in the time signature. Lynne wrote it as he needed a lively up-tempo number about it being 'nice to have something to hold onto' or anticipating 'something over the horizon that's good so just keep holding on 'til you get it'. Once completed, he decided it would be the most logical first track. It was released as a promotional single in Britain, physical singles having become largely a thing of the past, Record Store Day limited editions and the like excepted. Nevertheless, according to feedback from Sony UK and BBC Radio 2, there were stronger, 'more ELO-sounding' songs on the album.

2. 'Moment in Paradise'

A warm, relaxed summery song, with lyrics about a girl who 'floated out upon the wind, that blew my thoughts out into the night', or, more succinctly, in Lynne's own words, 'a tribute to Rosie (Vela)'. A gentle piano phrase, colourful lead guitar break, and Starr's steady drumming all contribute towards an enjoyable mellow sound. Musically, he aimed deliberately for an old-fashioned setting, almost like a fairground kind of sound, 'but really intimate at the same time'.

3. 'State of Mind'

One of the liveliest songs, and one of the few that features nobody apart from Lynne, is surely in part an act of homage to the record by his old mate, which helped to break him through to a wider audience. The guitar riff that dominates much of the song is built partly on a phrase that echoes the riff on 'Brontosaurus', The Move's 1970 Top 10 single and their first hit after he joined. The meaning of the song, he explained, was basically about making decisions 'that you might regret or might be pleased with but only depending upon what your state of mind is then'.

4. 'Just for Love'

A gentle, laid-back number with echoes of 'Across the Universe', opening with acoustic guitar before some extra backbone comes in about a minute later with rather Lennon-esque lead guitar. A false ending is followed by another guitar solo and airy vocal harmonies, which take about a minute to fade. The song's message is purely a simple one: 'To people who haven't got a personal happiness. You know, maybe one's just around the corner'.

5. 'Stranger on a Quiet Street'

Probably the most autobiographical song on the album, this was about his original meeting with Rosie. Their paths first crossed when he was working with the Traveling Wilburys and she played a little piano for them while they were socialising together, although she was not on any of the recording sessions. A few years later, they met again by chance in a restaurant, and it reminded him of meeting somebody on a quiet street. Rosie sang backing vocals, but they also became an item for a while. Soulful electric piano and steady beat almost suggest a dance number on first listen.

6. 'In My Own Time'

An old-fashioned song that sounds like a throwback to sixty years or more. An old-fashioned orchestral introduction, strings, and a swaying doo-wop rhythm bring The Inkspots, The Platters, and others to mind, with Rosie Vela ('naughty tap-dancing Spanish lady' as it says on the CD insert credits), speaking some lines in Spanish. What she is saying is not easy to understand, but it has been identified by one source as '*Y la biblioteca, ¿donde está?*' ('And the library, where is it?'); Lynne is not the first songwriter to have a chuckle at the thought of listeners looking for hidden meanings where there surely are none.

7. 'Easy Money'

Alongside 'Alright', this is the most immediately commercial, most rock 'n' roll number on the album. With Starr on drums, it is a gutsy rolling bluesy tune, with a chord pattern and rhythm similar to that of Billy Swan's 'I Can Help', and not for the first time in Lynne's songs, a basically twelve-bar structure to the verses but with a departure from the pattern in the interlude. The pointed lyrics read as if they are directed at somebody—'the only time you ever cared was when you needed more'—and are thought to be a comment on the (by then laid to rest) ELO Part II situation or other ex-members who had gone out on the road playing the old hits. Just before the guitar solo, there is a slightly muffled 'Take it, Jeff!'—a private joke with one of the Jeffs calling out to another.

8. 'It Doesn't Really Matter'

Another song on which Lynne provided all voices and instruments, this mid-tempo tune with relaxed feel has definite overtones of Tom Petty and the Heartbreakers, and a powerful guitar solo takes the song up a gear. Lynne wrote it while on a beach in the Bahamas with Vela in a particularly peaceful frame of mind, as reflected in the lyrics.

9. 'Ordinary Dream'

This opens with strings and piano, again recalling some kind of homage to Lennon, and a strong hook in the chorus. After the second chorus the violins run riot again for a few seconds in a piece reminiscent of some of the passages on the first two ELO albums, and at the end of a comparatively mellow song, a dazzling break on lead guitar to finish. Although not released as a promotional single, this was Sony UK and Radio 2's main choice. Sony also favoured 'Moment in Paradise', while 'Ordinary Dream' continued to be played regularly on the radio for some time after the album was released.

10. 'A Long Time Gone'

Lynne wrote this song about his mother, after he and a friend had visited Birmingham together. He suggested that they both went to go and look at the place where he used to live as the houses were being demolished. By the time they had arrived, the bulldozers were there and half the street had gone, much to his regret as his mother had died in 1988: 'I saw this like two years ago and it was sort of connected—the two were connected in the fact that we hadn't said goodbye and now they're knocking down the place where I was so happy with her … when I was a little lad'. It opens with some unmistakable Harrison guitar, another slow dreamy song. The lyrics tell of memories of an old acquaintance and thoughts of 'doorsteps that shone in a bright summer sky, lay shattered and wasted since our last goodbye'.[11]

11. 'Melting in the Sun'

This one immediately evokes thoughts of The Traveling Wilburys' 'Handle With Care', not only in the opening rhythm guitar, but also with a vocal in the style of Harrison and Dylan. However, the melody is more complex, and a fine melodic guitar solo complements it to perfection. While recording it, Lynne experimented with a cheap Walkman tape recorder in order to get an old-fashioned rock 'n' roll sound where the microphone breaks up with distortion.

12. 'All She Wanted'

Heralding echoes of vintage Rolling Stones and of 'Ma-Ma-Ma Belle', this starts off with a rocking electric rhythm guitar, complemented by Harrison's slide. Two verses and choruses are followed by a brief respite without drums and with a touch of phasing, then a powerful slide guitar passage. Additional support in the rhythm section comes from Katayama's cello work.

13. 'Lonesome Lullaby'

Another experiment with retro styles, this track opens with a few seconds of guitar reverb, sounding like it was fed through a very small old guitar amp. Despite the title, this is no lullaby, but a slightly bitter number addressed to someone who 'pulled the wool over the eyes of everyone, maybe [they were] weak when [they] should've been strong' and saved themselves by saving nobody else. There are more retroisms—a few cello phrases recall early ELO, the lyrics 'cry baby cry' remind one of a Beatles' song of that title, and the last few seconds feature the guitar reverb once more.

Japanese Bonus Track

14. 'Long Black Road'

Initially released on the *American Hustle* movie soundtrack album, this is a more hard rocking track with heavy percussion and lyrics of defiance from a boy determined to make his own way in life despite being told he is going nowhere 'with [his] cheap guitar and [his] big long hair'. The bonus track here is in stereo, unlike the *American Hustle* version, thought to be in mono by mistake.

2013 Bonus Tracks

15. 'One Day'

A pleasant mid-tempo song, recorded in 2004, tells of looking forward to a brighter future: 'When I'm tired of doing time'. It has a kind of George Harrison feel, particularly with the lovely melodic guitar break.

16. 'Turn to Stone' (live)

Taken from the *Zoom Live from Television City* concert and barring the fadeout, it is a faithful reproduction of the original version.

2013 Japanese Bonus Track

17. 'Do Ya'

Also from the *Television City* concert, this follows the arrangement of the version on 'A New World Record', albeit with less prominent strings and no choir on the finale.

18. 'Lucky Motel'

A two-minute instrumental assumed to have been recorded in the 1990s or shortly thereafter, which starts off with ukulele, with keyboards, a Hank Marvin-style guitar solo and percussion coming in later. As a mid-tempo, waltz-like affair, the effect is similar to one of how The Shadows crossed with The Tornadoes might have sounded together in the 1990s.

2

ELO Part II

Electric Light Orchestra Part Two

UK:	Released 1991, Telstar, No. 34
US:	Released 1990, Scotti Bros
Current edition:	not available
Personnel:	Bev Bevan: drums, percussion, backing vocals
	Pete Haycock: lead and backing vocals, guitars, bass guitar
	Eric Troyer: lead and backing vocals, keyboards
	Neil Lockwood: lead and backing vocals
	Mik Kaminski: violin (track 5)
	Louis Clark: string arrangements

Recorded at The Mill Studios, Cookham, Angel Studios, Islington, Rich Bitch Studios, Birmingham, Fanfare Studios, Colorado, and Capitol Studios, Hollywood, 1989–1990
Produced by Jeff Glixman

Lynne was unreceptive to Bevan's proposal that they resurrect the group in 1988, and Bevan reformed them without him and Tandy. The album was recorded on both sides of the Atlantic with three new vocalists, two of whom were also seasoned session players and singers—Haycock, formerly of The Climax Blues Band, and Troyer, having worked with the likes of Billy Joel (his is the first voice heard on 'Uptown Girl') and Meat Loaf. Kaminski returned for one track only, but alongside Clark, Groucutt, and (very briefly) McDowell, he rejoined the group as a full touring member when the album was released in Britain in 1991, a few months after its American appearance. The group was now more of a democracy. As Bevan said at the time of their press launch, 'there is a lot of talent in this band, and we wanted to share it out'.[1] The obsession with synthesisers and drum programming, which had encroached over the last three albums, was conspicuous by its absence. They sold out gigs at home and abroad, playing rapturously received sets, mixing their own material and old favourites, but never completely won over the 'where's Jeff Lynne?' faction. Some of the album works well, although a few tracks fall into the 'pleasant but nothing special' category.

Tracks

1. 'Hello' (Eric Troyer, Bev Bevan, Pete Haycock, and Neil Lockwood)

The album begins with seventy-five seconds of a friendly song on which Troyer's vocal is backed largely by piano. The theme is 'great to see you again'—nothing more, nothing less. It serves as a prelude to 'Honest Men'.

2. 'Honest Men' (Eric Troyer)

The most lyrically weighty number on the album, maybe the equivalent twenty years on from the Woodstock generation's message of 'everybody get together and love one another'. Troyer sings lead on his song, written and recorded around the time of and possibly influenced by unrest around the Gulf and the disintegrating Soviet Union; it is set in a world where humanity is 'a stone's throw from Burning Hellfire, scoundrels and power-hungry liars', and a few upright honest souls are the solution. It is a patently sincere message, although some reviewers derided it at the time. Brisk keyboards and Clark's wonderfully extravagant soaring strings provide the backing. At just over six minutes, it is the longest track on the album, though edited to four minutes for release as a single; it reached No. 60 in Britain.

3. 'Every Night' (Eric Troyer and Ken Cummings)

With lead vocal by Lockwood, this boasts a heavier guitar to the fore. The lyrics are of ill-concealed lust and infidelity, complimented by a strong hook in the chorus, harmony vocals, more soaring strings, and forceful lead guitar just before the fadeout.

4. 'Once Upon a Time' (Bev Bevan and Pete Haycock)

Haycock takes lead vocal on a love song of regret about happier times as the narrator searches for his love's face among the crowd while knowing he has to rebuild his life and find somebody new. There is the sound of birdsong, and also what appears to be noise from a children's playground. Enlivened by strings and lead guitar break, it is pleasant in a middle-of-the-road kind of way.

5. 'Heartbreaker' (Bev Bevan and Pete Haycock)

Probably the standout track on this collection, this is introduced by clever sound effects—a clap of thunder, heavy rainfall, the sound of a car braking and somebody getting out, with a quick blast of the song's chorus as if played through a car radio. Gutsy guitar chords *à la* Rolling Stones or Bad Company are followed by Lockwood's vocal about a femme fatale who will lure the unsuspecting to heartbreak city. Clark's strings are excellent, as are the harmony vocals, powerful drumming, blistering guitar solo, and the long-overdue return of Kaminski on fiddle.

6. 'Thousand Eyes' (Eric Troyer)

Another inoffensive, if not particularly striking mid-tempo pop number that coasts along pleasantly enough with the help of piano and strings, though it does not really get into gear until the guitar solo. It was a non-charting single, and perhaps significantly the only song from this album to be included on the group's first live set, made up otherwise of Lynne-penned old favourites.

7. 'For the Love of a Woman' (Eric Troyer)

A pretty, if rather so-so middle-of-the-road love song with Troyer on lead vocal, sounding rather like a cross between Roy Orbison and Dean Friedman.

8. 'Kiss Me Red' (Billy Steinberg and Tom Kelly)

The only non-original track, formerly recorded by Cheap Trick and penned by the partnership responsible for 1980s hits from Madonna, Heart, The Bangles, and Whitney Houston, among others. One of the standout tracks, with Lockwood on lead vocal, it is a veritable showcase for strings and vocal harmonies, resulting in a bombastic string-fest towards the fade.

9. 'Heart of Hearts' (Eric Troyer)

Yet another mid-tempo song—in the style of American contemporary names such as Toto and Styx—again finds Troyer on lead vocal; the track makes good use of the strings and lead guitar.

10. 'Easy Street' (Bev Bevan and Pete Haycock)

This brings a little grit, even anger, to the proceedings. At first, the lyrics sound like it could be a riposte to a former boss (let listeners draw their own conclusions)—having had enough of being pushed around, and 'tired of the man giving me such a hard time'—until, later on, the inference that the message comes from somebody who is moving on, has the key to the big city, has found the right girl, and is on easy street. Haycock's vocals and incisive guitar suggest a touch of the blues, not a million miles from Gary Moore, and appropriate string flourishes here and there.

The Moment of Truth

UK:	Released October 1994, Edel
US:	Released July 1995, Curb
Current edition:	not available

Personnel: Bev Bevan: drums, percussion
Eric Troyer: lead and backing vocals, keyboards
Kelly Groucutt: bass guitar, vocals
Phil Bates: lead guitar, vocals
Mik Kaminski: violin
Louis Clark: orchestral keyboards and orchestral arrangements
London Session Orchestra, leader Gavyn Wright: strings
Hossan Ramzy: percussion

Recorded at Carriage House Studios, Connecticut, Great Linford Manor Studios, Milton Keynes, Whitfield Studios, London
Produced by Stephan Galfas

Line-up changes saw Groucutt and Kaminski fully integrated as full members in the studio as well as on stage, alongside Bates, whom they had known since he was a member of Trickster (a group who had signed to Jet Records and supported ELO on tour some fifteen years earlier). The album followed in similar vein to that of its predecessor, although it was more ambitious in forging links in the past with an overture, underture, and three short interludes, thus immediately creating a connection with *Out of the Blue* and other albums of that era—to say nothing of a front cover illustration of a light bulb shattering (as it was their last studio recording, in retrospect some might have considered this prescient). Nevertheless, if ELO Part II's debut was a little unsure of itself and inconsistent, the second time around, they sounded more in control and the standard was higher. Once again, reviews varied and chart success was lacking due partly to distribution problems on the part of new label Edel.

Tracks

1. 'Moment of Truth (Overture)' (Louis Clark)

This makes the listener wonder if another concept album is on its way, but here any resemblance with thoughts of a second *Eldorado* ends. Even so, it is a splendid modern-day homage to the Savoy Opera overtures and others of their kind.

2. 'Breakin' Down the Walls' (Phil Bates)

As with many songs on its predecessor, stylistically the song itself slips comfortably after its dramatic strings introduction into the flow of mid-to-late 1980s pop-rock, but with a stronger song and more of a hook in the chorus. Those eager for comparisons might cite Tears for Fears, but that is no criticism. The final chorus is followed by a reprise of the introduction.

3. 'Power of a Million Lights' (Eric Troyer)

Thirty seconds or so of piano and acoustic and electric guitars herald a song that calls to mind The Moody Blues. The chorus is a stirring one with full-on romance: 'I can feel the power of a million lights when I see your eyes turn bright'. It shares a common theme with 'Telephone Line' and 'Calling America'—that of losing contact with a loved one. Troyer explained the fantasy aspect of the song in that the man is talking on the phone, thinking about the feeling he gets when he sees her, and decides to hook up televisions, computers, and power lines from the neighbours in order to travel through space and be with her once more.

4. 'Interlude 3' (Louis Clark)/5. 'One More Tomorrow' (Bev Bevan, Mik Kaminski and Phil Bates)

Thirty seconds of fairly spirited strings lead into a powerful pleading ballad, of the kind that Tom Jones once regularly made his own. When the group previewed it at a concert for the first time, the audience could not possibly have heard it before, but by the end, they were singing along.

6. 'Don't Wanna' (Eric Troyer)

With its simple thunderous drums introduction and rough and ready chords behind the vocals, this more raw rocky number is reminiscent of early Kinks and The Who, but the vocal harmonies and hook on the chorus transform it into something even more powerful, while the lead break with storming guitar and violin interplay add another dimension and add up to one of the album's strongest tracks.

7. 'Voices' (Phil Bates and Mik Kaminski)

A mid-tempo and rather unsatisfying number, leaning a little too heavily on Bad Company's 'Feel Like Makin' Love'. The strong hook on the chorus and the guitar solo go some way towards rescuing it.

8. 'Interlude 2' (Louis Clark)/9. 'Vixen' (Kelly Groucutt)/10. 'The Fox' (Kelly Groucutt)

A twenty-second breathing space with strings—similar to the earlier 'Interlude', but a little slower—is followed by a five-second snippet, Groucutt's whisper of 'Ooh, you little vixen, you!'. Then comes a song that OrKestra, most of whose members had joined from ELO in the 1980s and now returned to ELO Part II, had performed regularly on stage. With dramatic strings and drums but no other instruments (the hunting horn was somehow overlooked), it tells the story of the hunt from the point of view of the fox—who escapes and lives to fight another day.

11. 'Love or Money' (Eric Troyer and Phil Bates)

A pleasant enough ballad, which threatens to become a little nondescript until the soaring chorus and suitably majestic guitar solo.

12. 'Blue Violin' (Kelly Groucutt and Mik Kaminski)/13. 'Whiskey Girls' (Bev Bevan and Phil Bates)

The first piece is basically an interlude, little more than a minute in length, with keyboards and (naturally) violin, and a chant: 'Play for me your saddest melody'. It acts as a curtain-raiser for the album's star performance, a straight-ahead rock number opening with a sharp stabbing guitar chord or two and the cowbell marking time, then launching into a steady beat. There are shades of The Doobie Brothers' 'China Grove', and a tale of ladies who love to party, while some neat touches of organ and violin add extra colour.

14. 'Interlude 1' (Louis Clark)/15. 'Twist of the Knife' (Kelly Groucutt, Bev Bevan and Phil Bates)

Clark's next 'Interlude', one minute's worth of stately, almost funeral march-fare on strings, leads into a pop-rock-country-ish number, sounding like a cross between Asia and The Eagles. Sturdy acoustic guitar chords give way to a fairly brisk verse that morphs into a slower chorus.

16. 'So Glad You Said Goodbye' (Bev Bevan, Eric Troyer and Phil Bates)

Some strong interplay on guitar and keyboards on a Toto-like number enliven this story of good love gone bad.

17. 'Underture' (Louis Clark)/ 18. 'The Leaving'

Nearly three minutes of instrumental farewell, which would not have sounded out of place on *Out of the Blue*, are followed by a few seconds while somebody evidently left the tape running as everyone left the studio.

3

Jeff Lynne's ELO

Alone in the Universe

UK:	Released November 2015, Columbia, No. 4
US:	Released 2015, Columbia, No. 23
Personnel:	Jeff Lynne: vocals, guitars, piano, bass guitar, drums, keyboards, vibes Steve Jay: tambourine, shakers Laura Lynne: background vocals (tracks 2 and 9)

Recorded at Bungalow Palace Studios, 2014–2015
Produced by Jeff Lynne

After *Zoom*, Lynne returned to producing other artists, notably George Harrison and his last album *Brainwashed*. Rumours surfaced regularly of further solo releases, finally realised in 2012 with *Mr Blue Sky*, an album of rerecordings of the hits (and one previously unreleased track) by Lynne on his own, credited to ELO, and *Long Wave*, a solo album featuring cover versions of old favourites, mostly from the 1940s and 1950s (see p. 62).

Fourteen months after the Hyde Park concert came the first album credited to Jeff Lynne's ELO, again an almost entirely solo venture. It consists of new songs, all tightly focused and arranged, with none hitting the four-minute barrier—a return to the days when the classic single said everything it needed to in two and a half minutes flat. 'When I was a Boy', 'When the Night Comes', 'One Step at a Time', and 'Ain't it a Drag' were all download singles in Britain and regularly played on BBC Radio 2. While one might miss the interaction between different musicians, which enriched so much of ELO's earlier work, and perhaps another full-tilt rock 'n' roll song, the absence of synthesisers and drum programming result in a much more human-sounding set. With singles having entered the download era and the days of purchasing 7" or 12" of vinyl on the high street in their thousands a thing of the past, it barely mattered. The best chart performance for an ELO record since the early 1980s proved the point.

Not for the first time, Lynne showed his knack for taking elements from his back catalogue, yet without it sounding like an inferior cut and paste from his greatest hits—not to say also absorbing even little trademark motifs from his heroes and from those he had worked with before, such as John Lennon (albeit posthumously, if one counts co-producing the last two Beatles' singles from Lennon's raw home demos) and Roy Orbison. This is an album chock-full of solid songs, rather than epic numbers with the little experimental twists that were his stock-in-trade around four decades before. If it may sound a little relaxed, lacking in up-tempo numbers and too easy-listening on first acquaintance, the lovingly well-crafted musical settings and singing shine through and show it for the endearing work its creator intended it to be.

Tracks

1. 'When I was a Boy'

Released as a download single in September 2015, six weeks ahead of the album, this is a wistful look back at Lynne's Birmingham childhood and teenage years. It reflects on how good the carefree early years were, growing up and listening to a little crystal-set radio with headphones, when there were few worthwhile pop stations generally playing about an hour's worth on Saturday night, then becoming a rebellious music-loving teenager spurning conventional employment to follow the pop dream. He admitted it was his most autobiographical song ever. He said that the words just wrote themselves, 'whereas normally I'd sweat them out and chain myself to my desk'. Musically, it is a ballad with warm synthesised strings and echoes of 'Imagine' or his Beatles-produced 'Real Love', with a spark provided by the Harrison-like lead guitar break.

2. 'Love and Rain'

In a nod to blues and reggae, this is another of those songs that can be traced in a line of descent back to 'Showdown'—even if this time the lyrics no longer tell us it is raining all over the world—or even 'Last Train to London', via the guitar, albeit at a slower, more laid-back pace. The main riff sounds like a clavinet, but it was played on a Telecaster guitar. With lyrical references to 'steppin' out', to say nothing of rain yet again, there is also an obvious reference to a song and a concerto on *Out of the Blue*. A blues flavour comes with the guitar solo eighty seconds in, while Lynne's daughter Laura adds backing vocal.

3. 'Dirty to the Bone'

In the tradition of 'Evil Woman', lyrically speaking, this is another song possibly directed at some former female friend or lover. There are bitter references about how she will 'drag you down until you drown in sorrow', rather at odds with the pretty tune and lovely vocal harmonies. *The Guardian* called the album 'an excellent return', with only one *faux pas*: 'The clumsy, Whitesnake-worthy lyrics' on this track being 'rooted a little too firmly in the 70s'.[1]

4. 'When the Night Comes'

The second song to be released for download ahead of the full album, and one of the few on the album to feature a string section, comes very close to a mellow brand of reggae, with shades of early Police. Not for the last time, there are allusions to the narrator being on his own when the night comes: 'And I'm here all alone'.

5. 'The Sun Will Shine on You'

A slow song full of lush strings, a steadily underpinning piano, and warm vocal harmonies. Lyrically, it has an emotional message of learning how to fall, how to cry, and how to turn from the darkness in order to reach a brighter dawn on the other side. Lynne commented that it was basically about trying to give his daughters support on a bad day. It was a difficult time for them after his divorce, and he was telling them that one day 'the sun will shine on you if you just do what you've got to do. Just face up to it and try to get over it'.[2]

6. 'Ain't It a Drag'

Lynne realised he needed more of a rocker in the set as, in his words, he 'was in the mood to do almost a Mersey beat number'. Brisk and full of hooks in the tune, not to mention sunny Beach Boys-type harmonies and a snappy, beautifully concise guitar solo, it is probably the most instant song of all on the album. It was a download-only single, heavily promoted on Radio 2, though one line, 'the shit hits the fan', was discreetly altered to 'it all hits the fan' in the interests of airplay.

7. 'All My Life'

Arguably the most stirring ballad of all, even considering the competition, this is a pure simple love song with no hidden messages and another succinct guitar solo nestling with the strings. Had it been a song on a Beatles album, this is doubtless the one that established solo artists would have been queueing up to cover, *à la* 'Yesterday'.

8. 'I'm Leaving You'

Here comes the unashamed Roy Orbison moment, a song Lynne wrote as an affectionate tribute to his late friend and fellow Wilbury, a deliberate attempt to come up with something Orbison would have written with his early songwriting partner Joe Melson. He admitted that 'the tune could've been a Roy Orbison song' and 'a great one if he had sung it': 'But of course, I'm a bit late for that by about twenty-eight years. He was such a lovely guy anyway that I wanted to give him a nod on this album'.[3] A close listen might detect a touch of Orbison's 1963 classic 'In Dreams'. There is also a small but clever lyrical twist, comparable to that in the closing moments of 'Oh Pretty Woman' ('what do I see, is she walking back to me?'), but in this case, it is a less happy one. Towards the end, the narrator turns the tables as he tells his formerly loved one that she may be leaving him on his own, but there is something she should know before she goes: 'I found somebody new and I'm leaving you'.

9. 'One Step at a Time'

With its slightly disco vibe, this is another contender for the album's most commercial moment. Lynne admitted he needed more up-tempo songs, and this had some very intricate chords in the verse, 'which [he liked] a lot, because it's sort of old-fashioned music but with a regular rock and roll beat'. There is a shuffling rhythm buoyed along by keyboards and guitar, backing vocals from Laura Lynne, and a crisp guitar solo. Also, from a musical perspective, there is a suggestion of the 'Evil Woman' chord sequence forty years on. As for the theme, it is evidently another bittersweet song on communication problems and a relationship going awry. 'Talk to me, with the sadness in your eyes,' as he sings, asking not to be given the silent treatment, so they can take it one step at a time.

10. 'Alone in the Universe'

The title track can be seen as partly a lament for lost love and about the feeling of heartbreak and solitude, as the title indicates. However, it was allegedly inspired by an article Lynne had read about the *Voyager 1* probe leaving the solar system to become the first man-made object to enter interstellar space. He asked, 'how lonely can you get?' It can therefore work on two levels: one, the lone astronaut, an isolated Major Tom figure from 'Space Oddity' almost half a century later; and two, a lonely man on earth, pure and simple. He cited the influences as some of his favourite songs when he was growing up, those by Del Shannon and Roy Orbison, whose songs (especially those of the latter) were so often about loneliness. Some reviewers suggested that this caps the album as a concept record, a metaphorical journey, from the era of childhood lovingly evoked in 'When I was a Boy', through songs of failed relationships, sadness, isolation, and coming full circle to the resignation and acceptance of the situation in the title track.

Bonus Tracks

Two more songs appeared only on deluxe versions of the album, featuring superior packaging with a hologram cover design. The Japanese deluxe version included these, plus a third.

11. 'Fault Line'

Sounding more like a demo than a completed song, this two-minute rockabilly shuffle is a straight-ahead, no frills number with simple guitars, bass, and drums, as well as the most basic of solos—almost like a 1950s Carl Perkins tune. Tune-wise, it is practically a rewrite of the old Leadbelly tune 'Midnight Special'. The impression is of a great track in progress that would have benefited from a little more work.

12. 'Blue'

Almost a Paul McCartney moment in its unabashed simplicity, this features the simplest of lyrics, with a tune dominated by minor chords, ethereal harmonies, and attractive guitar solo. Lynne had long had a preoccupation with the colour—'blue is the world, blue is the night'—as evidenced by several of his previous song titles.

Japanese Bonus Track

13. 'On My Mind'

A restrained song of love and loss—no matter what she says, goes part of the lyric, he will still believe in her and can't forget her. The verses are gentle, even pleasing in tone, but offset by a gritty Elvis Costello-sound-alike voice on the interlude.

4

Additional Tracks from Other Albums

The Night the Light Went on in Long Beach

The only live album issued by the group prior to disbanding in 1986 was initially released in 1974 in Germany and other overseas territories, but not in Britain or America, partly as it was intended mainly as a promotional tool for countries unfamiliar with the group. Only an unfinished rough mix was available, and they were dissatisfied with the sound. In 1985, a better quality mix was discovered in the record company vaults and it was released in Britain, but soon deleted. In 1998, a remastered version appeared on CD. For technical reasons, only two tracks from *On the Third Day* were featured, as well as an extended version of 'Showdown' and 'Day Tripper'.

Bevan said that he had 'never been a fan of live albums and this was no exception', and Lynne presumably shared his opinion. The contrast between this and the 2013 album below is remarkable. This set reveals an act that was not interested in playing note-for-note renditions of their greatest hits, but a progressive group keen to add a few twists to familiar songs as well as play the odd song they had not recorded—and never would—on singles or studio albums.

'Day Tripper' (John Lennon and Paul McCartney)

A rare cover version from their 1974 touring schedule, their rearrangement of the old Beatles favourite opens with a couple of bars of the introduction played on synthesiser, to be replaced by the riff from the original, though with the benefit of added strings. After two verses, they use a theme from Mozart's 'Piano Sonata in C Major', and following a subsequent verse, a snatch from Handel's 'Arrival of the Queen of Sheba', followed by with a few seconds of Kaminski playing the three-note introductory riff from the Rolling Stones' '(I Can't Get No) Satisfaction'.

The group played another interesting shotgun marriage of Beatles, Stones, and classics on several dates of their tour of Britain and America between November 1975 and April 1976, a segue of 'Let's Spend the Night Together', Grieg's 'Piano Concerto in A Minor', and, to finish, a section from 'The End' from side two of *Abbey Road*. Poor-quality bootlegs have been noted, though no recording has yet been officially released.

'10538 Overture'

The live version deviates slightly from the recorded one, with a few synth whooshes and whirls taking the place of the parts played initially on French horn and also in that, almost three minutes in, the opening chord sequence from 'Do Ya' is played. They often featured it live this way over the next two years or so, as evidenced by a recording of their performance at the New Victoria Theatre, London, in June 1976, initially for television but also later released on video and subsequently DVD under the title *Fusion*. Audience reaction resulted in their recording 'Do Ya' again, as related above (see p. 43) on *A New World Record*.

'Mik's Solo/Orange Blossom Special' (Ervin T. Rouse)

Kaminski's short violin spot turns into a country hoedown, a tune written in 1938 about the passenger special of the same name. Recorded by Ervin and Gordon Rouse a year later, it is sometimes known unofficially as the fiddle player's national anthem. This also remained in ELO's stage show for some time afterwards.

'In the Hall of the Mountain King' (Edvard Grieg)/'Great Balls of Fire' (Otis Blackwell and Jack Hammer)

The second song sounds much tighter, rather faster (and almost three minutes shorter) than the 1972 live version. It makes do without the additional interludes on strings between vocal phrases at unexpected moments, and Lynne takes a few interesting liberties with the chord sequence near the end of the song, which adds extra colour without losing momentum or having to alter the basic tune. It inevitably ends again on the first two bars of 'Roll Over Beethoven', which provided them with an entrée for their performance of the final song.

Mr Blue Sky: The Very Best of Electric Light Orchestra

Released under the group name in October 2012 on the Frontiers label, simultaneously with the solo album *Long Wave* (see p. 98), this was a collection of rerecordings of old material made by Lynne at his Bungalow Palace Studio over the previous few years. He maintained that, with the benefit of modern technology and providing all vocals and instrumentation himself, he could improve on the originals. The result was new versions of eleven of the old hits, namely the title song, 'Evil Woman', 'Strange Magic', 'Don't Bring Me Down', 'Turn to Stone', 'Showdown', 'Telephone Line', 'Livin' Thing', 'Do Ya', 'Can't Get it Out of My Head', and '10538 Overture', plus the previously unissued 'Point of No Return'. It entered the British album chart at No. 8 (America No. 118 (Billboard)). The Japanese release featured a bonus track, a live recording of 'Twilight', while the iTunes release added four tracks, 'Ma-Ma-Ma-Belle', 'Rockaria!', and acoustic performances with Richard Tandy of 'Steppin' Out' and 'Can't Get it Out of My Head'.

'Point of No Return'

The only previously unreleased song has a very George Harrison feel, as if tailor-made for *Cloud Nine*, *Brainwashed*, or even one of the Traveling Wilburys albums. There is a twang to the rhythm guitar and keyboards are kept well in the background for extra colour without becoming dominant. It has been suggested that the lyrics might suggest travelling, but it is more likely about a failing relationship between two people who 'could only run' but never walk, only shout but never talk. The theme of communication breakdown between partners is similar to that of several lyrics of the songs on *Balance of Power*. It was, however, inspired partly by the global banking troubles in the first decade of the new millennium. Lynne admitted that it was 'the general mood of the time like 2009 or something. It's a story about a guy who's not very pleased with lots of things that are going on'.[1]

Electric Light Orchestra Live

Released in 2013, this album comprised eleven tracks from a performance at CBS Television City, Los Angeles, in May 2001. Apart from Lynne, the only member of the old group still in the line-up was Richard Tandy. Augmented by Rosie Vela (backing vocals), Marc Mann (keyboards, guitar, backing vocals), Gregg Bissonette (drums), Matt Bissonette (bass guitar), Peggy Baldwin, and Sarah O'Brien (cellos), they played a twenty-one song set in a show released on DVD, intended to open the *Zoom* tour, which was cancelled due to poor ticket sales. A live CD was issued by Frontiers in April 2013, containing eleven tracks from the concert, all songs first released between 1973 and 1983, with none of the seven featured numbers from *Zoom*. Two previously unreleased studio tracks, recorded by Lynne in his entirety presumably during or after the *Zoom* sessions but credited to ELO, were added.

'Out of Luck'

A rockabilly number, this sounds like a deliberate and effective attempt to recreate the sound of early Elvis Presley or Gene Vincent. No-nonsense 1950s rock 'n' roll, with vocal and guitar soaked in echo, and Jordanaires-like harmonies on the interlude, which breaks briefly out of the old three-chord format.

'Cold Feet'

Closer to American AOR, a tinkling keyboard introduction springs a gentle joke in the opening line: 'Is that you out last night—you got cold feet'. The music throughout is largely keyboards, apart from the guitar break, and the melody is based largely on minor chords. A pleasant song, it is let down slightly by the rather repetitive lyric.

Afterglow

A forty-seven-track, three-CD compilation released in America in 1990 and deleted soon afterwards, this included most of the hits, excluding those from *Xanadu* for contractual reasons. It was the first to include several of the non-album B-sides, which have so far not appeared on any subsequent official release, and so far, it is the only one containing the following three tracks on the third disc of the set initially intended for the *Secret Messages* double album (see p. 62).

'Hello My Old Friend'

Lynne had originally planned *Secret Messages* as ELO's final work, ending with a song serving as a bookend to '10538 Overture'. At almost eight minutes long, this epic was the longest and most ambitious track recorded by ELO since *ELO 2* in 1973. As one of the most complex, thoughtful songs from the group's later period, despite its lack of instant easy-on-the-ear appeal, it was superior to much of the material that did appear on the penultimate album.

Lyrically, it is one of Lynne's most impressive, a farewell to his old town and his old group. It takes the form of an affectionate, if not unreservedly enthusiastic memoir-cum-travelogue about his early days in Birmingham, with mentions of skinny dogs and beer crates, high rise tower blocks with their panoramic views of trains and cars all around, cooling towers, and factory gates. Lest this implies a negative or jaundiced visual sweep from the rooftops, in the last verse he mentions sunset with 'pretty rainbows over your majestic towers' and how he could stand for hours and hours 'to feel your earth beneath my feet'. There is another reference to his earlier days in the sound of street vendors calling out ''Spatch and Mail', the *Dispatch & Mail* being a local newspaper. Musically, it is a slow, swirling tune shrouded in almost ambient keyboards, with something of a Pink Floyd atmosphere, and at the same time—almost inevitably—of 'Strawberry Fields Forever', lyrically and musically. About three minutes in, there is a two-minute instrumental section from guitar, drum patterns, and strings, which has elements of the group's bold classical-styled 'Fire On High', the coda from 'A Day in the Life', and music from an old science-fiction movie. Towards the fadeout, schoolchildren's voices singing *'Frère Jacques'* can be heard behind the lead vocal, made outside the studios in Holland as it reaches a crescendo, 'I am the Walrus'-like, with the help of a touch of the descending guitar riff from '10538 Overture', and a brief section of the string passage from 'The Diary of Horace Wimp'.

Prior to the start of sessions for the album, Lynne rehearsed some of the new songs with the group. Some of the results were taped and found later in the record company vaults, titled 'The Garden Rehearsals'. Included were this song and another, 'Motor Factory', with lyrics written from the viewpoint of staff at the Longbridge industrial complex, featuring the sound of hammers hitting a lathe for the percussion, and revving engines in the chorus and lyrics penned from the perspective. This latter one never progressed further than rough demo stage, then the vocal was erased in favour of another about a disillusioned rock 'n' roll singer named Johnny. It was not completed, but some of the ideas used in it survived in 'Rock 'n' Roll is King'.

'Mandalay'

An enigmatic, lyrically dark piece that may or may not be about a time-honoured legendary figure or the city; this track is steeped in references to and pictures in words of tracing footsteps down multi-coloured avenues, a breeze that flows up high into the blue (instead of 'out of the blue' this time), and, above all, Mandalay 'of the misty eyes'. The vocals are heavily soaked in echo, against a portentous wash of synthesisers and programmed rhythms, with a song that suggests the mood (and in places melody) of Jimmy Webb's 'MacArthur Park'.

'Buildings Have Eyes'

Like 'Night in the City', the lyrical mood of this song is one of claustrophobia in a city where 'the windows watch you as you walk along', the air is chilly under a moonlit sky, and, as the title indicates, there is no hiding place. Musically, it is mid-tempo, with tinkling synths and programmed drums, with an almost catchy hook, anticipating several of the songs that would appear on *Balance of Power*. It was first released on the B-side of 'Secret Messages', the second single from and title track of the album, though not as a bonus track on the remastered CD in 2001.

Flashback

A fifty-three-track, three-CD compilation released in Britain and America in 2010, and this time with Lynne's involvement, containing most of the hits (although, again excluding the *Xanadu* material), and a few previously unreleased numbers plus incomplete fragments. Several of these were recorded in Wisseloord Studios, Hilversum, Holland, in 1982 with Richard Tandy, after the *Time* tour as brief acoustic sound checks while Lynne was looking for a suitable studio to record the album that would become *Secret Messages*. The long-form package includes a beautifully produced illustrated book, including Lynne's thoughts on each track.

'Grieg's Piano Concerto in A Minor' (Edvard Grieg)

Given the title 'Ballbuster' on the tape box, initially recorded in 1982 and finished in 2000, this engaging three-minute collision between rock 'n' roll and the classics, with no strings in sight (or sound), features Lynne on drums, Tandy on piano, and both on guitars. After the stately, melodramatic introduction on piano, the drums come in fifteen seconds later and it sounds like a hybrid of Love Sculpture's 'Sabre Dance' and The Shadows' 'Ghost Riders in the Sky', with a brief stop about halfway through to vary the pace before it all starts again. According to Tandy, it was purely 'a fun thing' when they walked in to the studio to test the acoustics, with the drums at one end and the piano the other. Both launched into their respective instruments, had it down on tape within ten minutes, worked out the chords on guitars, and did a couple of overdubs.

'Tears in Your Life'

This began as a song from the *Secret Messages* sessions in 1982, initially recorded with vocal sung through a vocoder, perhaps to make more of a contrast with the basically similar 'Letter from Spain'. Left incomplete at the time, Lynne returned to it in 2000, replacing his lead vocal with a three-part harmony. Slow and melodramatic, with a moody keyboard riff and plenty of echo, it is a simple number with a Middle Eastern-like melody and little in the way of lyrics apart from the title. Lynne said that the tune he had had in mind did not fit, so he 'did some chopping about, changed the sequence of all the instruments and then sang it in three part harmony'.

'Great Balls of Fire' (Otis Blackwell and Jack Hammer)

Taken from the version on *The Night the Light Went on in Long Beach*, with 'In the Hall of The Mountain King' edited out.

'Xanadu'

This 2000 rerecording is a no-frills performance with mainly acoustic guitar, piano, and drums. Towards the end, a few touches of lead guitar take the place of the string flourishes that were to be heard on Olivia Newton-John's version, and the result sounds more akin to Lynne's style from the George Harrison and Traveling Wilburys era. Lynne said he had always liked the song, and that it had been 'sung brilliantly' by Newton-John, but he just fancied the idea of completing his own version.

'Indian Queen'

Just under a minute long, this is a fragment from 1973. As Lynne said: '[It is] a little demo that I never got around to finishing'. There is little more to it than a slow chant, muffled vocals, and possibly acoustic guitar, although the sound quality is poor and it is difficult to make anything out really clearly.

'Love Changes All'

A mid-tempo song with acoustic guitar and piano, and call-and-respond vocal, this was based on the 'Xanadu Overture' and started during sessions in 1980 as, to quote Lynne, 'another track that's taken twenty years to finish because only now could it be finished'.

'Helpless'

Another song begun in 1982 before the *Secret Messages* sessions and completed in 2000, with a similar mood and style to 'Xanadu'.

'Who's That?'

Not a song so much as a ninety-second fragment from 1982 of Lynne and others fooling around in the studio, joining around the piano for a singsong with silly voices', in the vein of The Beatles' madcap 'You Know My Name (Look Up the Number)' with a majestic orchestral chord at the end. It is based around a raspberry blown and 'played' using the pitch-altering capabilities of a Fairlight CMI synthesiser.

The Other B-Sides

'Drum Dreams'

Unique among the group's catalogue in never being included on an album at the time or on any subsequent compilation, this was on the B-side of 'I'm Alive', the first of the singles from *Xanadu*. As the title suggests, it is basically a drum instrumental, a disco-era answer to the old Sandy Nelson number 'Let There Be Drums' (which Bevan had recorded and released as a solo single in 1976) or Cozy Powell's 'Dance with the Devil'. The percussion is supplemented with a small amount of guitar, keyboards, and syn-drums, and 'Xanadu' chanted by a chorus for the last minute. Lynne has sole credit as a composer, although one might have expected Bevan to be cited as co-writer at least. Having been used in the movie during a major dance sequence, its omission from the soundtrack album, both the original and the 1998 CD reissue, is surprising.

'ELO Megamix'

The B-side of the 12" single of 'Getting to the Point', released in July 1986, featured a ten-minute megamix by Paul Dakeyne of DMC (Disco Mix Club), including 'Don't Bring Me Down', 'Sweet Talkin' Woman', 'Livin' Thing', 'Calling America', 'So Serious', 'Shine a Little Love', 'Twilight', 'Turn to Stone', and 'Hold On Tight'. With parts of each number segued together to a dancefloor beat, it fitted in with the general craze for mid-1980s megamixes in the wake of Stars on 45's success with disco medleys about five years earlier, and with British record buyers' brief obsession with Jive Bunny and the Mastermixers' product that dominated the singles chart in 1989. It was assembled without Lynne's approval and has never appeared on any compilation.

5

Solo Albums

Jeff Lynne

Armchair Theatre

UK:	Released July 1990, Reprise
US:	Released July 1990, Reprise
Current edition:	Frontiers
Personnel:	Jeff Lynne: vocals, guitars, bass, piano, keyboards, autoharp, percussion, drums George Harrison: acoustic guitar (tracks 1, 3, 5), slide guitar (tracks 3, 5, 9); backing vocals (tracks 1, 3) Richard Tandy: acoustic guitar (tracks 1, 2), piano (tracks 5, 9), backing vocals (tracks 2, 5, 9, 10) Mette Mathiesen: drums (tracks 1-4, 6-10), percussion (tracks 1, 2, 6, 10); backing vocals (tracks 5, 9, 10) Phil Hatton: backing vocals (tracks 1-5, 7, 9, 10) Jim Horn: saxophones (tracks 1, 2) Michael Kamen: string arrangements (tracks 1, 9) Hema Desai: operatic vocals (track 1), classical Indian vocals (track 6) Jake Commander: backing vocals (tracks 2, 5, 9, 10) Sireesh K. Lalwani: percussion (tracks 3, 6), violin (track 6) Vikram A. Patil, Nellai D. Kanan, Fateh Singh Gangani: percussion (tracks 3, 6) Dave Morgan: backing vocals (tracks 3, 5, 9, 10) Rita: saw (track 5) Sheila Tandy: backing vocals (tracks 5, 9, 10)

Ashit Desai: classical Indian vocals (track 6)
Del Shannon: backing vocals (track 10)
Recorded 1990 at Raindirk at Posh Studios, Birmingham, Lynne's home studio
Produced by Jeff Lynne

After putting ELO on indefinite hold for three years (at a time when it seemed he had put the name behind him for good) and producing for other artists as well as helping to form The Traveling Wilburys, Lynne was offered a contract for a solo album by Warner Bros largely on the strength of his work on *Cloud Nine*. It was a world away from the last few ELO albums, featuring a more stripped-down Jeff Lynne and friends. In his words, it was 'all done by hand', with no sequencing or digital work—a proper record with drums, bass, guitars, and pianos, plus occasional saxophone and strings. Having been 'through all that digital period, learning how to be a typist, pushing all these buttons', he was now reverting to a warmer, more natural sound.

The album featured eight new Lynne compositions, plus three cover versions, a forerunner of his full nothing-but-covers collection on his subsequent solo album *Long Wave*. An updated edition on Frontiers Records in 2013 added two bonus tracks.

Tracks

1. 'Every Little Thing'

The first single and a minor British hit, reaching No. 59, begins with a brisk backbeat, with shades of Lynne's production on Harrison's 'Got My Mind Set On You' and a song reminiscent of The Miracles' 'Going to a Go-Go', with emphasis on the rhythm guitar and saxophone. Those with longer memories instantly recognised the title (though not the song) as identical to a Lennon-McCartney song on the Beatles' 1964 album *Beatles for Sale*. An extended 12" version lasting almost eight minutes, with the first two minutes almost entirely instrumental and some percussive breaks just over five minutes in, was also briefly available.

2. 'Don't Let Go' (Jesse Stone)

A faithful, brisk version of the old rockabilly song that was first an American hit for Roy Hamilton in 1958. The lead, rhythm guitars, and bass drive it along solidly with a few well-paced stops and restarts, and suitably wild saxophone solo about halfway through, making it the liveliest burst of rock 'n' roll on the record.

3. 'Lift Me Up'

The second British single but not a hit is a more ethereal number, with some attractive vocal harmonies and strong hook in the chorus. Lynne said that it was a deliberate attempt to write an 'up' song, instead of a 'down' one: 'Jolly ones are very hard to write because they become smug almost'.

On sale Friday, week ending October 3, 1970 9

Move becomes ten-piece Electric Light Orchestra

YEAR-OLD PLAN NOW FULFILLED

ROY WOOD'S ambitious plan to augment the Move into a ten-piece ensemble named the Electric Light Orchestra has at last been realised. The project — first reported in the NME last year — finally reached fruition this week with the news that the enlarged outfit is currently rehearsing and routining. The line-up includes a string quartet, french horn and two miscellaneous instrumentalists — plus Jeff Lynne on piano and lead guitar; Roy Wood on bass, acoustic guitar and oboe; and Bev Bevan on drums.

Main function of the new orchestra will be for concert appearances, and it is expected to undertake a series of dates in this country towards the end of the year, when it has a sufficiently large and well-rehearsed repertoire. The band will also record, and its first release is expected to be an album.

It is, however, stressed that the Move will continue to operate as a small group. In fact, it has a new single scheduled for release by Regal Zonophone next Friday (9) — the Roy Wood composition "When Alice Comes Back To The Farm." A new Move album will follow in mid-November.

Above: A cutting from *New Musical Express*, 3 October 1970, announcing the birth of ELO.

Below: ELO, early 1972.
Front, left to right: Roy Wood; Jeff Lynne; and Bev Bevan.
Centre, left to right: Wilf Gibson; Hugh McDowell; and Bill Hunt.
Rear, left to right: Richard Tandy; Trevor Smith; Brian Jones (crew); Andy Craig; and Richard Battle (crew).

Above left: ELO on stage, with Richard Tandy and Roy Wood.

Above right: ELO on stage, with Jeff Lynne and Roy Wood.

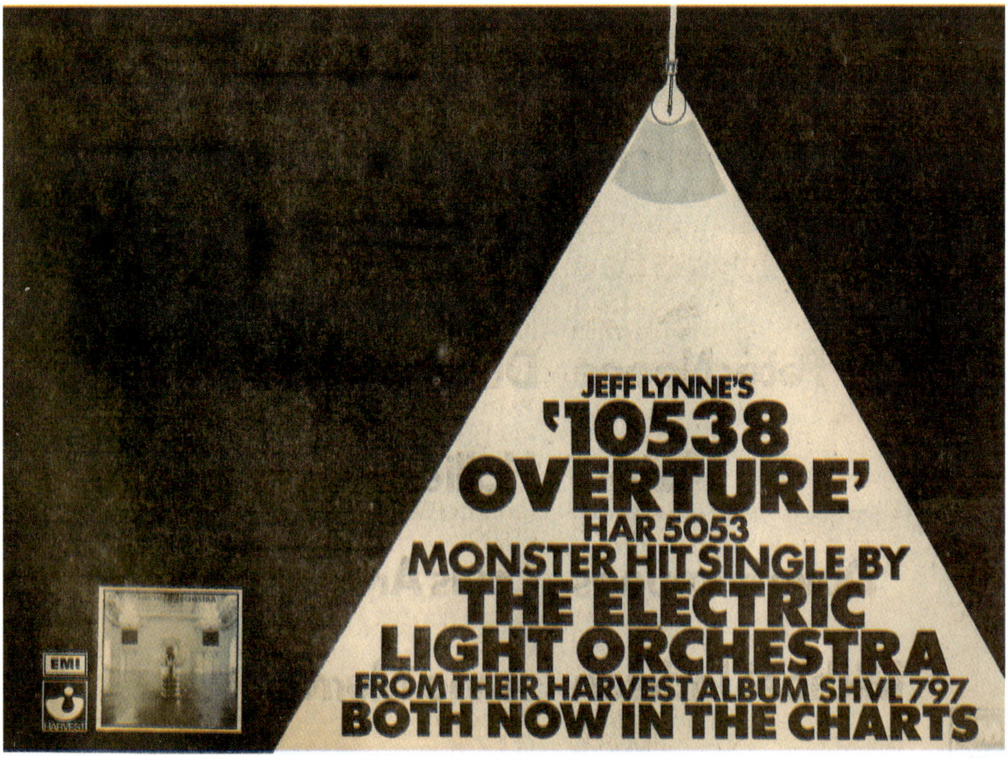

'10538 Overture', a British music press advertisement, August 1972.

Above left: 'Roll Over Beethoven', the French picture sleeve.

Above right: ELO, 1973, the line-up that recorded *ELO 2*.

'Showdown', a British music press advertisement, September 1973.

Above: ELO, 1973, miming 'Showdown' on BBC TV's *Top of the Pops*, with sound engineer Rick Pannell on cello, and new violinist Mik Kaminski.

Below left: ELO, 1973–74, shortly after cellist Hugh McDowell had rejoined.

Below right: 'Ma-Ma-Ma Belle', the sheet music.

Above left: ELO, 1975, with new bass guitarist Kelly Groucutt.

Above right: 'Rockaria!', the sheet music.

Below: ELO, 1976.

Above: Jeff Lynne with Baron George-Brown, former Deputy Leader of the Labour party, at the Capital Radio Music Awards, March 1978. (*Diamond Picture Library*)

Below left: A British music press advertisement for 'Wild West Hero' single, May 1978.

Below right: 'Wild West Hero', the sheet music.

Above left: ELO, 1978, during the *Out of the Blue* tour. (*Croydon Music Archive*)

Above right: 'Sweet Talkin' Woman', 7-inch coloured vinyl.

Below: ELO on stage during the *Out of the Blue* tour, 1978. (*Croydon Music Archive*)

Above: ELO, 1979, now a quartet and minus the string players, while recording *Discovery*.

Left: 'All Over the World', the sheet music.

Opposite above left: ELO, 1981, while recording *Time*.

Opposite above right: ELO, 1983, shortly before the release of *Secret Messages*.

Opposite below: 'Rock 'n' Roll is King', the sheet music.

in U.S.A.
Rock 'N' Roll Is King
Words and Music by
JEFF LYNNE
As recorded by E.L.O. on Jet Records

Above left: *Secret Messages*, the 7-inch picture disc.

Above right: ELO, 1986, the trio who recorded *Balance of Power*.

Left: Jeff Lynne on stage, 1986. (*Diamond Picture Library*)

Above left: Jeff Lynne, about 1987, with from left Slim Jim Phantom (Stray Cats), Dave Edmunds, Brian Setzer (Stray Cats), George Harrison, Duane Eddy, and Bob Dylan. (*Alan Smith Photographs*)

Above right: Jeff Lynne and George Harrison, 1987, while working on the latter's album *Cloud Nine*. (*Alan Smith Photographs*)

Below: ELO Part II, 1991. *Left to right*: Kelly Groucutt, Hugh McDowell, Eric Troyer, Pete Haycock, Mik Kaminski, Bev Bevan, Louis Clark, and Neil Lockwood.

Groucutt and McDowell did not appear on the first album and Kaminski was only on one track, but they all played live together, with McDowell being the first to leave.

Electric Light Orchestra 30th Anniversary

ELECTRIC LIGHT ORCHESTRA
(Remastered & Enhanced)
30TH ANNIVERSARY LIMITED EDITION
Release Date: 12 November 2001
Catalogue No: EMI Harvest 533 3722

"This is a pretty wacky album, so innocent yet so bold. It goes to some really strange places."
Jeff Lynne, 2001

"This was certainly the birth of E.L.O... I would have to say that together, Jeff and myself made my original dream into a reality. If I am to be honest, I sincerely love him for it."
Roy Wood, 2001

In celebration of the 30th Anniversary of the original release of **ELO's** first album (3 December 1971) EMI Harvest release a special remastered and enhanced CD of their groundbreaking, eponymously titled debut, **The Electric Light Orchestra** with two bonus tracks. Limited edition copies will include a bonus disc, **First Light** which contains 12 previously unreleased tracks (one of which is hidden) including alternate quadraphonic mixes, together with newly discovered and previously unheard session outtakes and live material. The enhanced facility has been designed by Abbey Road Interactive and contains original and unpublished album artwork, rare and unpublished live, studio and promotional photographs and much more.

This superb release, compiled by **Rob Caiger** (of ELO fan club Face The Music & band archivist) with the help of **Jeff Lynne** and **Roy Wood**, has been two years in the making and once you see the quality of the finished copies, it's hard not to see why.

For more info: www.ftmusic.com

"A NEW SOUND, A NEW CONCEPT..."
EARLY ELO HISTORY BY JOHN VAN DER KISTE

In 1966 **The Move** signed their first record contract and it took little time for them to establish themselves as one of the most successful singles acts around, their first and third releases reaching No. 2 and the second at No. 5 during 1967. But lead guitarist and songwriter **Roy Wood**, already dissatisfied with the limitations of their line-up, hankered after the idea of another band playing more ambitious songs with additional instruments. When they released their eponymously-named debut album in March 1968, its 13 tracks included not only both sides of the group's previous two singles and the customary cover versions from the stage set, but also three new songs relying less on conventional guitar-bass-drums backing and more on baroque-style string quartets, woodwind et al.

Roy: It was the early Move albums that really gave me the idea for the Electric Light Orchestra. We had to bring in session men, and they never really did play the parts we wanted from them - they played off the dots with no feeling at all - so I thought wouldn't it be nice, with the sort of songs I was writing then, to reproduce the sound on stage. I've always been interested in the lower, the heavier end of the orchestra, the 'cellos and basses, and I thought it would sound less Mantovani if we didn't have any violins. That's why we formed the string quartet largely of 'cellos - one fiddle just to play solos and things.

After the acrimonious departures of bassist **Ace Kefford** and then **Trevor Burton**, who had switched from rhythm guitar to bass, the recruitment of new bassist **Rick Price**, and a difficult US tour in 1969, manager Peter Walsh embarked on a 'Clean Up The Move' campaign, forsaking the heavy rock, axe-

Bev Bevan, Roy Wood, Jeff Lynne - ELO 1971

Left: Face the Music supplement, 2001, announcing the thirtieth anniversary reissue of *Electric Light Orchestra.* (*By kind permission of Parlophone Records/Face the Music*)

Below: First Light, a limited edition bonus CD from the thirtieth anniversary reissue of *Electric Light Orchestra.* (*By kind permission of Parlophone Records/Face the Music*)

Opposite above: The Lost Planet, a limited edition bonus CD from the thirtieth anniversary reissue of *ELO 2.* (*By kind permission of Parlophone Records/Face the Music*)

Opposite below: Harvest Showdown' 2001, a CD featuring material from ELO, The Move, Wizzard, and Roy Wood. (*By kind permission of Parlophone Records/Face the Music*)

HARVEST RECORDS IN ASSOCIATION WITH SHARD END MUSIC INC. PROUDLY PRESENT
THE
LOST PLANET
Starring
THE
ELECTRIC
LIGHT
ORCHESTRA

HARVEST
SHOWDOWN
ELO
THE MOVE
WIZZARD
AND MORE!
EARLY CLASSICS ON HARVEST RECORDS 1970 - 1973

Left: *Boulders*, 2007, a card promoting the reissue of the remastered version with bonus track on CD.
(*By kind permission of Parlophone Records/Face the Music*)

Below: A British music press advertisement for Michael de Albuquerque's *We May Be Cattle But We've All Got Names* album, 1973.

Opposite: Jeff Lynne's ELO onstage, 2015. 'Roll Over Beethoven' remained the time-honoured encore.
(*By kind permission of Jeff Cooper*)

ROLL
OVER BEETHOVEN
HAR 5063
THE ELECTRIC LIGHT ORCHESTRA

Above left: An advertisement for Jeff Lynne's ELO *Alone in the Universe* tour, 2017.

Above right: Jeff Lynne on stage with Jeff Lynne's ELO, 2015.
(*By kind permission of Jeff Cooper*)

4. 'Nobody Home'

A moody mid-tempo song with some interesting, almost Elvis-sounding vocals, Hammond organ, and a Beatles-inspired guitar solo.

5. 'September Song' (Kurt Weill and Maxwell Anderson)

This opens with some relaxed acoustic and Hawaiian slide guitars, and brushes on the drums, with Lynne crooning the vocal in equally laid-back style. Cocktail piano tinkles delicately in the background, and the guitar takes a solo further on.

6. 'Now You're Gone'

The most adventurous track on the album; this is a mid-tempo number with a strong undercurrent of Indian classics, emphasised by an Indian violin solo. The arrangement was inspired by Lynne's attendance with George Harrison at a Ravi Shankar concert in England, and his asking the two singers afterwards if they would come and record some music at his house. The song, he said, was very chordal: 'With lots of harmonic tension. In Indian music, one note is a drone, and the musicians and singers tend to play around that. Anyway, the song had an open area in it, and the vocalists sang this amazing raga that should have fitted over one note but actually blended into the chords'.[1]

7. 'Don't Say Goodbye'

Particularly steeped in the after-effects of Lynne's work as a member of The Traveling Wilburys, this gentle number sounds remarkably like Harrison (though it is one of the tracks on which he does not appear), both vocally and in the song construction and chords themselves, not to say the guitar solo as well. The chorus also has a distinct echo of Roy Orbison and Del Shannon, breaking into a marvellous falsetto at one point near the end.

8. 'What Would it Take'

A strong hook on the guitar introduction and an infectious chorus, on a song that would not have sounded out of place on the first Traveling Wilburys album.

9. 'Stormy Weather' (Ted Koehler and Harold Arlen)

A song from 1933 and the third cover version on the album is another relaxed crooning number. The choir and strings are kept well in the background, and Harrison's guitar is particularly noteworthy here.

10. 'Blown Away' (Jeff Lynne and Tom Petty)

Without doubt, this is the album's finest ballad, with lyrics co-written by Tom Petty and backing vocals by Del Shannon, a song of love and loss with choral vocals enhancing a delightful hymn-like melody on the chorus. With a nod to another rock 'n' roll hero of the same era, the guitar solo has something of a flavour of Duane Eddy, whose then most recent album also benefited from Lynne's input as collaborator and producer on some tracks.

11. 'Save Me Now'

Lynne on his own, accompanied just by acoustic guitar, simple keyboards, and background vocals. The message of the song, the shortest on the album at less than two minutes, is told from the earth's point of view, deliberately written like a nursery rhyme.

Bonus Tracks

12. 'Borderline'

This was omitted from the original album but included on the 12" and CD single of 'Lift Me Up', an uncharacteristically folksy song with Lynne accompanied only by acoustic and bass guitars and a touch of country-ish lead. Cheerfully repetitive in the tradition of the best school songs, it sounds like the kind of number Leadbelly made popular for children to sing along with.

13. 'Forecast'

A doomy number opening with the sounds of thunder and lightning, then portentous piano chords, and a touch of drums and electronic keyboards. Lyrically, it takes metaphors of deep depression and bad weather ahead together. After three minutes, it comes to an end, with a brief pause followed by a few more seconds of atmospheric meteorological sounds.

Long Wave

UK: Released October 2012, Frontiers, No. 7
US: Released October 2012, Frontiers, No. 133
Personnel: Jeff Lynne: lead and background vocals, guitars, piano, bass guitar, drums, keyboards, vibes
Recorded 2010–2012 at Bungalow Palace Studio, Los Angeles
Produced by Jeff Lynne

Lynne's first album of cover versions was thus named because all the songs featured were ones he had heard on long wave radio as a child growing up in Birmingham. They took him back 'to that feeling of freedom in those days and [summoned] up the feeling of first hearing those powerful waves of music coming in on [his] old crystal set'. His father always had the radio on: '[Some of the songs had] been stuck in my head for fifty years. You can only imagine how great it felt to finally get them out of my head after all these years'.[2] Easy-listening fare rubbed shoulders with rock 'n' roll classics. Eleven other so-far unreleased recordings were made at the same sessions, namely 'The Sunshine of Your Smile', 'You'll Never Walk Alone', 'Stardust', 'Sally', 'All Alone Am I', 'Sleep Walk', 'Some Enchanted Evening', 'Night and Day', 'My Prayer', 'Goodbye My Love', and 'Saturday Night at the Duckpond'.[3]

Recording material from the pre-rock era, as about half of it was, presented him with the challenge of rebuilding the songs from the ground up. This involved getting to the basic song itself in each case and liberating it from the original arrangement, to the extent of listening carefully to the recordings of each one and learning them all: 'It probably took a hundred listens before I could actually understand the song, because of all of these big arrangements. When you get to where you have this tunnel hearing on, then you start listening to one instrument at a time. It is great because you can learn how all the parts go; the piano part, the bass part, the string part. You don't want to just copy them; you want to make them your own'.[4] He freely admitted that, like many a music lover from his generation, he had acquired the taste for songs over the years that he had not enjoyed at first—and in some cases positively hated, only learning how to love them in the two years or so before recording the album as he learnt how to play them.

The scene on the front cover of the sleeve is Sherborne Street, Birmingham, about 1950. It features a photoshopped Lynne, with his guitar just visible, standing in the doorway of a shop, above which the sign reads 'Fender'.

Tracks

1. 'She' (Charles Aznavour and Herbert Kretzmer)

By far the most recent song on this album, it was a British No. 1 hit for Aznavour in 1974 (around the time that ELO were recording *Eldorado*), thanks to exposure through use as the theme for the TV series *Seven Faces of Woman*. It had a second lease of life as a British No. 19 in 1999 with Elvis Costello's version on the soundtrack of the movie *Notting Hill*. Lynne's version features a backing of mainly acoustic guitar, piano, and drums, with vocal harmonies and electric guitar on the interlude.

2. 'If I Loved You' (Richard Rodgers and Oscar Hammerstein)

This love song was a show tune from the 1945 musical *Carousel*, filmed in 1956. The many cover versions recorded since then include one by Annie Haslam of Renaissance on her 1977 solo album *Annie in Wonderland*, produced by Roy Wood—who played most of the instruments throughout. Lynne croons to a lush backing of mostly strings and piano. He said he never dreamed in a million years that he would be singing something like that, 'but it was actually the most marvellous thing, the most fun [he] ever had recording it'.

3. 'So Sad (To Watch Good Love Go Bad)' (Don Everly)

A British No. 4 and American No. 7 for The Everly Brothers in 1960, Lynne called the original 'two-part harmony at its best', and strove with good effect to get an authentic sound on the lead guitar as well as reproducing the brothers' vocal harmonies very well.

4. 'Mercy Mercy' (Don Covay and Ronald Miller)

An American Top 40 hit when released by Covay in 1964 with the then little-known Jimi Hendrix on guitar, this song became well-known in Britain after The Rolling Stones covered it on their third album, and Lynne performed it on stage regularly with The Idle Race. Revisiting the song over forty years later, he follows the original very closely, down to the touches of falsetto vocal.

5. 'Running Scared' (Roy Orbison and Joe Melson)

Having always idolised Roy Orbison, it was inevitable that Lynne would choose to record one of his songs, this being a British No. 9 and American No. 1 (his first in his homeland) in 1961. Tackling 'these old, beautiful songs', he said, meant that they had to be treated with total respect, even more so once he had met Orbison and become a friend. During a conversation one night, the latter told him that 'Running Scared' was the favourite song from his own back catalogue. He knew he could never come close to the original, but that he would do the best he could for his own version. This is arguably the best track on the album. Lynne not only replicates the original arrangement faithfully with guitars, piano, drums, and a touch of strings, but his voice also does credit in the closing crescendo to his hero's remarkable semi-operatic range.

6. 'Bewitched, Bothered and Bewildered' (Richard Rogers and Lorenz Hart)

From the 1940 Broadway musical *Pal Joey*, which became a Frank Sinatra movie in 1957, the original was one of the records that Lynne's father owned and would play regularly. Lynne said: 'This had some of the most beautiful chords of any song ever. You listen to it and you realise just how clever a song it really is'. The smooth arrangement of keyboards, strings, and unobtrusive harmony vocals give this a laidback, dreamy quality and make it one of the most successful 'easy' songs on the collection.

7. 'Smile' (Charles Chaplin, John Turner, and Geoffrey Parsons)

Based on an instrumental theme written by Chaplin for the soundtrack of his 1936 movie *Modern Times*, inspired by Puccini's *Tosca*, the piece had lyrics added by John Turner and Geoffrey Parsons in 1954, with the message of a bright tomorrow, just as long as the listener will smile. The first version to be recorded with lyrics, by Nat King Cole, was a British No. 2 and American No. 10 hit that same year. It has since also been covered by Eric Clapton, Diana Ross, and Michael Jackson. Lynne sings it pleasantly enough and adds a short guitar break before the final verse.

8. 'At Last' (Mack Gordon and Harry Warren)

Written for the 1941 movie *Orchestra Wives*, it became known best through a 1960 version by Etta James. It is as close to blues and jazz as Lynne comes on the album, with a gentle swing to the rhythm and its finest moment coming about twenty seconds before the end with a dramatic final vocal crescendo and a coda, which is a combination of guitar and string effects.

9. 'Love is a Many-Splendoured Thing' (Sammy Fain and Paul Francis Webster)

Written for the 1955 movie of the same name, a British No. 2 and American No. 1 for The Four Aces, Lynne's pleasantly relaxed version swings with a slow bluesy feel, enjoying a lift with the harmony vocal part towards the end.

10. 'Let It Rock (Chuck Berry)'

A minor American success for its writer in 1960, it was a British No. 6 hit in 1963; it was subsequently recorded by several others, including The Rolling Stones, Dave Edmunds, Bob Seger, and Motörhead. The lyrics tell the story of a group of workers on the railroad in Alabama who are suddenly warned by the foreman to move off the tracks at once as an off-schedule train is coming from less than 2 miles away. Lynne copies the guitar licks and piano faithfully on what is the shortest song here, a little under two minutes.

11. 'Beyond the Sea' (Albert Lasry, Charles Trenet, J. Zeino, and Jack Lawrence)

Written as 'La Mer' by Charles Trenet and first recorded by Roland Gerbeau in 1945, it was later adapted and became a swing tune with additions by Lasry, Zeino, and Lawrence. Of all the versions by other artists since then, the one by Bobby Darin (a British No. 8 and American No. 6 hit in 1959) is probably the most familiar. Lynne said the song contained 'thousands of chords, big fast bass, non-stop movement from start to finish', and he played all the brass and woodwind parts on his 1974 Les Paul.

Japanese Bonus Track

12. Jody (Del Shannon and Max Crook)

Originally recorded by Del Shannon as the B-side to his transatlantic 1961 No. 1 'Runaway', this was written about his daughter (whose second name coincidentally was Lynne). The new version is a respectful cover which faithfully follows the arrangement of the original, a gentle song in more or less waltz tempo, dominated by guitar and keyboards.

Roy Wood

Boulders

UK:	No. 15, Harvest
US:	No. 176 (Billboard), United Artists
Current edition:	EMI
Personnel:	Roy Wood; lead, harmony and backing vocals, electric, acoustic and steel guitars, bass guitar, piano, drums, percussion, mandolin, cittern, bouzouki, banjo, cello, double bass, brass, saxophones, bassoon, recorders, harmonica, water bowl John Kurlander: harmonium (track 1)

Recorded 1969–1971 at Phonogram Studios and Abbey Road Studios
Produced by Roy Wood

Wood began recording *Boulders* about three years after The Move was formed. Some of the material was developed from ideas that had been influenced by the use of new instrumentation, which he had never previously had the opportunity to experiment with while recording within the confines of a small group. He also had several songs that he felt were unsuitable for the group or for other artists. Although a number of other acts recorded his compositions for release as singles from 1968 onwards, only Amen Corner had any success—their version of 'Hello Susie' reached No. 4 in 1969—and he may have lacked the self-confidence to try and pitch some of them elsewhere.

It was a genuine solo album on which he provided all lead and backing vocals and instruments, apart from a harmonium played on the first track by an Abbey Road Studio engineer, and he produced it as well as painting the cover self-portrait, left unfinished on the recommendation of EMI staff. The result is a remarkably eclectic collection, especially in view of the fact that it is entirely the work of one person. Several genres are covered, from gospel to pop-folk ballads, from 1950s rock 'n' roll and bluegrass to Irish jigs, and one experimental, very ahead-of-its-time number—it was all done with good humour. There is a sense that everything is slightly tongue-in-cheek with often amusing lyrics. To quote one reviewer: 'He steadily pumps out incredibly catchy, if sometimes derivative melodies, and makes the album enjoyable as a "roots rock encyclopaedia" and as a true picture of his own inner fantasies and artistic soul in forty minutes'.[5]

Release was delayed partly because of his busy schedule with The Move, ELO, and subsequently Wizzard, partly as the first Move album was the only one to chart on Britain and came out nearly two years after completion. When it was remastered and reissued on CD in 2007, Wood commented in the booklet notes that it was 'old, but still weird enough to be different'. He also says that, if he could have done so, he would have called it '*Bollocks*', but in those days, he would not have got away with it. Most of Wizzard's records were renowned for their heavily overdubbed, slightly distorted, everything-but-the-kitchen-sink wall of sound. This is not the case on *Boulders*, where everything to be heard is as clear as the proverbial bell.

Tracks

1. 'Songs of Praise'

A few seconds of the warm tone of a harmonium to open with are joined by acoustic guitar, tambourine, and drums on the opener. It is a joyous, even uplifting gospel song, with Wood's lead vocal supplemented by many multi-tracked Roy Woods on an almost surreal choral backing. Submitted as a possible Eurovision Song Contest entry when The New Seekers were chosen to represent the United Kingdom in 1972, it was one of the final six to be shortlisted, although it came sixth out of six in the order of voting. It later became the B-side of 'Dear Elaine', and was also released as a single by Dutch group Husky.

2. 'Wake Up'

Plaintive, quite high-pitched vocals, backed by acoustic guitar, recorders, and cello are the main instruments on this gentle, folksy tune. It also features the eccentric percussion effect of stereo water splashes in a bucket performed faithfully by Roy, who took the advice of studio engineer Alan Parsons and wore a yellow sou'wester as he did so in order to get into the spirit of things.

3. 'Rock Down Low'

A few seconds of deep bass and high treble choral vocal and recorder, taken from the final track 'Dear Elaine' and played on reverse tape, segue into a snatch of rock 'n' roll, backed with a rhythm section of electric guitar, saxes, cello, and some playful flourishes on the piano. Instead of a Chuck Berry-style guitar break, saxes and cello are the main instruments.

4. 'Nancy, Sing Me a Song'

This returns to the folk-pop vein with acoustic guitar, cellos, and choral backing vocals. Even a slightly daft chorus refrain of 'Nancy, Nancy, sing me a song, something to make my hair grow long', sounds more gloriously playful than merely silly, which it might have done in the hands of a lesser talent.

5. 'Dear Elaine'

The album's loveliest song and hit single, reaching No. 18, features a lute (or acoustic guitar sounding like one), with a delightful mini-orchestration of choral harmonies, cellos, and recorders. It has been described as 'Tudor folk', and you can almost close your eyes and hear it playing in the background of a sixteenth-century costume drama. Percussion is kept at bay until drums enter behind the final verse.

6. 'All the Way Over the Hill/The Irish Loafer (and His Hen)'

This brings yet more acoustic folksiness, but to ring the changes, about halfway through, the cellos are joined by what sounds like a jazz break played on guitar-sitar for the instrumental break. It then returns to the song, and just as the last chorus finishes, a drum roll announces a minutes'-worth of Irish jig on violin and cello.

7. 'Miss Clarke and the Computer'

This is Wood's own favourite track; on first listen, it could be mistaken as a romantic tale of lost love, until it becomes apparent that the lyrics are quite surreal—about a robot developing feelings and falling for the lady engineer who comes to fix him, who is then afraid of her disassembling him because of some inner problems. The vocals of the song are electronically enhanced or distorted, gradually slowing down to nothing at the end, like a vinyl record switched off and coming to a full stop with its finale of 'Miss Clarke … don't take my heart awaaay!' in a deep bass rumble—apparently, illustrating the final words spoken by the robot before the screwdriver ends his life. Instruments include Welsh harp, string bass (ushering in a few seconds of relaxed jazz shuffle instrumental in the break), glockenspiel, and sitar. It is interesting to consider that it was recorded around 1971–72, years before PCs and laptops, when a computer was the size of a large desk.

8. 'When Gran'ma Plays the Banjo'

This is the nearest the album comes to a novelty number, and it was the first—largely ignored—single, released in January 1972 about eighteen months before the album. Wood said he released it thus because his mother liked it, although *New Musical Express* reviewer Danny Holloway called it a lame attempt to match Ray Stevens of 'Bridget the Midget' fame in the comedy single stakes. It finds Wood turning into a real mid-west cowboy, with transatlantic vocal twang, almost like a British John Fogerty. Gran'ma may have silver hair, the song's lyrics tell us, but when she goes to a festival she puts the others to shame with her bluegrass skills, not least 'cousin Luke', all fingers and thumbs, who makes a complete mess of his performance, is booed by the crowd and mutters that he hasn't played for a couple of weeks.

9. Rock Medley: 'Rockin' Shoes/She's Too Good for Me/Locomotive'

This segues three songs together. 'Rockin' Shoes' is pure country, foot-tapping rock 'n' roll with pedal steel guitar and could almost be from the mid-1950s Sun Studios catalogue. It leads into 'She's Too Good for Me', on which Wood sounds even more like the Everly Brothers than they did themselves. The song was originally started in the studio in 1968 with Trevor Burton during the days of The Move, and two short fragments appear on *The Move Anthology 1966–72* as 'Second Class (She's Too Good for Me)'. Both songs might be seen as a dress rehearsal for Wizzard's 'Introducing Eddy and the Falcons', released a year later, in which Wood wrote a complete album's worth of music, recorded in the style of several rock 'n' roll pioneers such as Gene Vincent, Neil Sedaka, Duane Eddy, and Del Shannon. Finally, 'Locomotive' revs up a gear or two into late Move and Wizzard territory, with more steel guitar and saxophones. Wizzard featured this song regularly on stage.

2007 Bonus Track

10. 'Dear Elaine' (rough mix)

This reveals very little difference with the issued version, apart from minor changes in the instruments, and a small amount of studio chat in some of the quieter moments—plus Roy at the end modestly asking the studio engineer 'Was that OK?'

Mustard

UK:	Released November 1975, Jet
US:	Released 1976, United Artists
Current edition:	not available
Personnel:	Roy Wood: lead and backing vocals, all instruments
	Annie Haslam: backing vocals (track 3)
	Phil Everly: vocals (track 9)
	Rick Price: choral vocals (track 6)
	Dick Plant: choral vocals (track 6)

Recorded at Phonogram Studios, De Lane Lea Studios, 1974–1975
Produced by Roy Wood

Recorded while Wood was simultaneously fronting Wizzard, this is a less commercial album than its predecessor. Although they failed to chart, two potential hit singles (both released as such) rubbed shoulders with melancholy ballads and the stirrings of his growing interest in jazz-rock. This came to fruition with the third and last Wizzard album *Mainstreet*, completed in 1976 but not released until 2000, partly as the record company thought it not commercial enough and partly as the tapes were missing presumed lost for many years. To some, *Mustard* is like Wood's own personal version of The Beach Boys' *Pet Sounds*, with a strong Brian Wilson influence on the melody and multi-tracked vocal harmonies on several tracks. As with *Boulders*, Wood provided the cover artwork, depicting himself in Wizzard garb with bagpipes and brightly checked trousers.

The album was reissued twice on CD, on the Edsel and Line labels, both with different bonus tracks from Wizzard and from Wood as a solo artist, including A- and B-sides not available on album at the time. These have long since been deleted.

Tracks

1. 'Mustard'

At ninety seconds long, this is something of a clever joke on the part of its creator. The opening few seconds, which sound less disturbing on CD than on vinyl, mimic a record stylus on an old scratchy disc, followed by a muffled jazz tune with horns and swing or dance-band era vocals by a female vocal group such as the Andrew Sisters, as if taken directly off an old 1930s 78 rpm disc, ending in fake applause.

2. 'Any Old Time Will Do'

The album's second single, released in August 1976, is a cheerful, uncomplicated pop number with piano, saxophone, and strong backing and harmony vocals.

3. 'The Rain Came Down on Everything'

A remarkable epic-like affair, this is probably the album's high point, and in terms of dramatic effect, it is one of the finest ballads Wood ever recorded. The first forty seconds evoke an atmospheric feel with eerie noises and choral singing, as if taken from a vintage sci-fi movie. This gives way to a series of stately piano chords later joined by French horn, and a slow, mournful tune with a medieval flavour, on which Annie Haslam provides backing vocal. It proceeds to a crescendo with harps, choral semi-Wagnerian operatic vocals, booming drums and harmonies into a finale with the sound effects of further rain and finally the roar of thunder. Notwithstanding the absence of strings, it has a certain ELO-like quasi-classical feeling.

4. 'You Sure Got It Now'

This also opens with an interesting soundscape, with a fade-in of a distorted siren, and saxophone effects, then an introduction of jazzy acoustic guitar and a verse of female swing vocals. Next comes a bluesy harmonica and slide guitar break, after which the song changes tempo with a brief sax break and a hard rock workout closest to some of the material on *Wizzard Brew*, with a touch of Robert Plant in the vocals. In five packed minutes, it manages to sound like several different acts—none of which are Roy Wood.

5. 'Why Does Such a Pretty Girl Sing Those Sad Songs'

A strong Beach Boys influence is at work here. Over the full four minutes, the effect is like that of a new 'Good Vibrations', with lead vocal, harmonies, and occasional falsetto evoking the style of the Wilson Brothers, and a brief dip in tempo just over halfway through.

6. 'The Song'

Another majestic ballad, beginning with a dignified section of choral vocals, piano chords, and what sounds like a mellotron. The joke, if such a word can be applied to a serious piece of music of this nature, is that only the first two minutes are taken up by the song, or rather vocals, and the remaining four and a half minutes are instrumental—more or less a funeral march. The instruments sound like mostly harp and organ, combining to produce a work of melancholy beauty.

7. 'Look Thru' the Eyes of a Fool'

This comes as a welcome return to straightforward pop. Issued as the album's first single at about the time that news of the disbanding of Wizzard broke, it is an infectious number driven along with piano, saxophone, and harmony vocals, and a neat sax and guitar break in the middle.

8. 'Interlude'

Eighty-five seconds of music begins as a slow dignified chant, then halfway through the drums usher in the same melody played on bagpipes, repeated several times until a short Beach Boys-like vocal harmony coda to finish with.

9. 'Get On Down Home'

The longest track at seven and a half minutes, this is Wood's own homage to Led Zeppelin. From a blast on the drums and a section with hard rock guitar and vocals, a John Bonham-esque two-minute drum solo is followed before an instrumental workout of which Jimmy Page would have been proud. As a song, it probably the least remarkable number on the album, but as Wood's one-man heavy metal outfit it works well. Not quite a solo effort, it includes vocals from Phil Everly in the middle section.

On the Road Again

UK:	Unreleased on vinyl
US:	Released 1979, Warner Bros
Current edition:	Warner/Parlophone, 2014, as part of *Roy Wood: Original Album Series*, also comprising The Move, *Message From The Country*, Electric Light Orchestra's first album, Roy Wood, *Boulders*, and Wizzard, *Wizzard Brew*. All five CDs have same track listing as original vinyl releases, without bonus tracks
Personnel:	Roy Wood: vocals, drums, saxes, cello, electric bass, guitars, percussion, sitar, mandolin, tuba, vibes, bagpipes, recorder, clarinet, violin, string bass Paul Robbins: backing vocals, piano, guitar, synthesiser, clavinet, recorder, percussion Billy Paul: saxophone Pete Mackie: backing vocals, bass guitar John Bonham: drums (track 3) Andy Fairweather-Low: backing vocals (track 1) Carl Wayne: backing vocals (track 3) Annie Haslam: backing vocals (track 8) Charlie Grima: congas

Recorded at Rockfield Studios, Monmouth; DJM Studios, London; Utopia Studios, London; Music Centre Studios, Wembley; Air Studios, London; Lee Sound Studios, Pelsall, 1977–1979
Produced by Roy Wood

On the Road Again, Wood's third solo album, is the least 'solo' of all four. On the others, he played almost every instrument and sang most, if not all of the lead and backing vocals. This is much more a group effort. The sleeve credits Rock Brigade, more or less a slimmed-down successor to the Wizzo Band, Wood's large and impossibly expensive-to-maintain jazz-rock combo that disbanded in 1978, shortly after a British tour was cancelled. Yet its core members are featured on several tracks, alongside friends such as former Move vocalist Carl Wayne, former Amen Corner vocalist Andy Fairweather-Low, and Led Zeppelin drummer John Bonham on one track each. Therefore, the contributions of others are much in evidence throughout. It was issued in America at the time and only obtainable in Britain on import. When Wood formed Roy Wood's Helicopters in 1979 for British live dates, a group including Paul Robbins, he included a couple of songs on stage that were from what he called 'the American album'. Note that saxophonist Billy Paul is not the late American soul singer.

It was reissued on CD by Wounded Bird in 2007, and subsequently as part of a five-CD boxed set in 2014, both without bonus tracks.

Tracks

1. '(We're) On the Road Again'

Issued as a single in 1979, this was more often seen on sale as a picture disc, and its failure to secure any radio airplay or chart position contributed to the cancellation of British release for the album. At a time when acts like The Bee Gees, Gloria Gaynor, and the Village People were topping the charts, more and more pop and rock acts were recording singles with a nod to the dancefloor. This has a thunderingly infectious call-and-respond chorus and also some great funky basslines and fills on the drums and cowbell in between the saxes and cello.

2. 'Wings Over the Sea'

Apart from the saxophone intro, this is almost a folk tune with its prominent accordion and mandolin. There are also some neat touches of slide guitar and a twangy Duane Eddy-like sound at times, alongside a tuba providing the kind of oompah-oompah beat once associated with Eurovision Song Contest entries.

3. 'Keep Your Hands on the Wheel'

This was released as a single in 1978. It is largely dominated, or at least powered throughout, by John Bonham's heavy drum sound—on one of the rare sessions he played for other artists. The song is built partly around a series of jazz chords, combined with a typically catchy chorus and also a typical Roy Wood surprise. Halfway through it changes tempo for about twenty seconds with a jig on the sitar, before returning to the main song with its ferocious drumming. Carl Wayne is one of the backing vocalists on the chorus.

4. 'Colourful Lady'

A jazz-rock workout from the last days of The Wizzo Band, the song lacks tune although the funky saxes add colour, as does the out-of-character Beach Boys-like a cappella vocal harmony passage at the beginning. The track is more or less a duet between Wood and fellow multi-instrumentalist Rob Mackie, who shares lead vocal and is partly responsible for the guitar solo at the end.

5. 'Road Rocket'

A return to the rock 'n' roll of Wood's 'California Man' era, sounding like a cross between Little Richard and Status Quo, complete with guitar soloing, saxes, motorbike, and some joyous barroom-style boogie on the piano.

6. 'Backtown Sinner'

This continues the hard-rocking edge. After a cello introduction, it goes more or less into Rolling Stones territory, with some mean lean Keith Richards-like guitar work weaving in and out of the sax and cello. Wood's new group Helicopters, formed not long afterwards, featured it regularly in their live set, with Paul Robbins singing lead vocal on stage though he did not on the record.

7. 'Jimmy Lad'

Wood ventures into contemporary Gaelic folk with a song making full use of recorders and mandolins as well as acoustic guitar and drums. Towards the end, it turns into the Scots Guards beating a retreat—or rather, Wood himself on bagpipes and military percussion, 'Mull of Kintyre'-style, with a bit of the old Stephen Foster song 'Oh Susanna' as it fades out at the end.

8. 'Dancin' at the Rainbow's End'

This was the second and final single by the Wizzo Band, released in 1978. It is a halfway house between jazz and pop, full of clever and unexpected chords, and clever interplay between lead guitars and saxophone, though let down a little by the lack of a strong hook.

9. 'Another Night'

A mainly acoustic number enlivened by plenty of percussion, congas, and bongos as well as a full drum kit, in addition to the usual harmony vocals, lead guitar, and sax.

10. 'Way Beyond the Rain'

At five and a half minutes, this is the longest track, the album's only ballad, and one of those sweeping, grandiose tunes Wood does so effectively. He contributes almost a full one-man orchestra on this one, building up a dense sound with violin cello, bass clarinet, and string bass, as well as guitars and drums. The instrumental passage, which takes up nearly all the last two minutes, has something of the dense, swirling soundscape of 'Strawberry Fields Forever'.

Starting Up

UK:	Released Legacy, February 1987
US:	Released Castle, 2006
Current edition:	Castle, 2001

Personnel: Roy Wood: vocals, all instruments except track 8
Louis Clark and Royal Philharmonic Violins:
string arrangement (track 8)

Recorded at Sinewave Studios, Birmingham; The Old Smithy Studios, Worcester; DJM Studios, London; Utopia Studios, London; Music Centre Studios, Wembley; Air Studios, London; Lee Sound Studios, Pelsall, 1977–1979

Produced by Roy Wood

Wood's fourth and last solo album came about four years after a period of playing British dates with his group Helicopters, recording briefly for the independent Cheapskate label, and a return to EMI followed by his departure when two singles flopped. During this time, like Lynne, he had adapted to the electro-pop era and experimented with drum programming, with a farewell to the days when he had been a one-man orchestra, multi-tracked choir, drummer, and everything else. His singles on the Cheapskate and EMI labels between 1980 and 1982 were ample evidence of this. Three singles and an album, initially to be titled *Imminent Attack*, resulted from a new deal signed with Legacy Records in 1985. Two singles appeared on the album, the seasonal 'Sing Out the Old (Ring In the New)', a rerecording of a 45 rpm he had first released in 1980, being omitted. Although not exactly a concept album, the sleeve design and three of the nine tracks suggest a strong preoccupation with the automobile world.

Wood admitted to disappointment with the final result. He had recorded everything without Dolby Noise Reduction as he felt it sounded warmer with a bit of analogue tape hiss. When the album was mastered, the company added Dolby Noise Reduction: 'To me it made it sound all digitised and electronic and horrible. It took the warmth out of it and I can't actually listen to it any more'.[6] It is hard to disagree with his view. The record sounds much sharper, and from a technical point of view, the sound quality may be better than the previous three, but colder and lacking in charm. As an example of mid-1980s electropop, it fitted the prevailing mood at the time, but now appears very dated. It was also recorded on a low budget due to record label pressure, and to this writer's ears at least, the album was short-changed by the constant drum programming and dance beats. The human touch—in other words, the presence of Wood (or indeed any other musician) attacking a proper drum kit with the appropriate gusto—is as sorely missed as the acoustic guitars, bagpipes, mandolins, and touches of folksiness that helped enliven the previous three albums. Moreover, some of it still seems like an attempt to merge the jazz-funk of the Wizzo Band (albeit in shorter songs, resisting the temptation to stretch everything out to seven minutes or more), without the pop hooks for which he had always been known. The result is for the most part a reasonable 1980s electropop album, but with too little of the individuality that had graced his earlier solo sets.

This was Wood's only album released on the Legacy label, which operated during the mid- and late 1980s and was distributed by PRT Records. It had no connection with Legacy Recordings, set up by Columbia, later Sony Music, for the reissue of archive material, including much of ELO's back catalogue.

Tracks

1. 'Red Cars Are After Me'

The first ten seconds of programmed beats sound like the production line in a factory, and they are then joined by guitar and saxophone. A catchy melody, skipping beat, clever lyrics, inventive percussion effects, and a swinging sax riff complement lyrics about paranoia and being stalked by vehicles of said colour, although the effect is light-hearted rather than eerie. All that holds it back is the same insistent drum track throughout, and it could have done with being supplemented or enhanced by genuine drums or other percussion effects, such as tambourine.

2. 'Raining in the City'

A very pretty tune, reminiscent of the Wizzard ballad 'This is the Story of My Love' strung delicately over and thunder and sax-laden backing track with a smooth-rising vocal relating the story of a man and his thoughts as he drives through a storm, physically or metaphorically.

3. 'Under Fire'

This was released as a single in 1985, with a short version on the 7". The 12" contained both the short version and a 'Mad Mix I', about forty seconds longer, with some additional reverse tape and echo effects, plus snatches of Beach Boys-like vocal harmonies in the first few seconds. This extended version is the one on the album, and it relies mainly on synthesiser and guitar with heavy drum programming. The lyrics concern a character who is trying to escape from being followed. At the end—as revealed by an audio clip uploaded to YouTube—comes the backwards message 'under fire and I'll never get out'. Does that remind you of anybody else?

4. 'Turn Your Body to the Light'

A prime contender for the funkiest track on the album opens with electropop keyboards, guitar work, Eastern-style intro, and solid backbeat. A few seconds of beats only are followed by a guitar solo, making for an interesting arrangement but lacking in pop hooks and tune.

5. 'Hot Cars'

This jazz-funk number sounds like a throwback to the Wizzo Band era, except, at a concise three minutes, it is far shorter than anything on the 1977 album. Although again lacking a genuine pop hook, the saxophone, guitar, and other instruments help to compensate by sustaining a worthwhile groove.

6. 'Starting Up'

Appropriately in view of the title, Wood turns in one of his best vocal, most urgent performances on this commercial up-tempo title track. The first few seconds feature a car being revved up into gear. Powered by a catchy brass riff and keyboard piece, it is punctuated after the second chorus with a brief guitar-sitar and percussion break, before reverting to the main song.

7. 'Keep It Steady'

Wood probably never aimed a song more directly at the electro-dance audience than this one, although it is overlaid heavily with Indian influences—Ravi Shankar meets the Human League or what? With heavy echo on the title phrase at the start, followed by a guitar-sitar introduction and percussion that sounds like a tabla—the drum programming and jazzy synths are prominent throughout. A saxophone solo and the occasional glissando on piano are topped by an urgent vocal in which Wood urges the listener 'if you feel like dancin', get up on the floor and keep it steady', capped by more funky synths. Perhaps more than anything else on the album, it may not have sounded like the Roy Wood that fans knew and loved, but although lacking in the pop stylings normally associated with him, this is the kind of record that one imagines might have found the right audience if promoted on release as a white label copy among club DJs.

8. 'On Top of the World'

A rock 'n' roll song in which the first two lines of the verse have a slight similarity to the Dave Edmunds hit 'I Knew the Bride'. Seemingly the only song on the album that Wood had ever played live, it had been part of the set list on the Helicopters gigs in 1982, when keyboard player Terry Rowley played a couple of bars of Tchaikovsky's Piano Concerto No. 1 in B flat minor as an intro. Wood used to introduce it on stage as a forthcoming single that had already been recorded with the violins of the Royal Philharmonic Orchestra, arranged by Louis Clark, but it remained unreleased until appearing as the B-side of 'Under Fire' in 1985. On the recorded version, the piano concerto except was replaced by a flourish from the violins was shorn of the piano concerto work, and a short guitar break about ninety seconds in brings a momentary slowing down of tempo before the subsequent verse. With Clark's input, it is surely the most ELO-sounding track Wood ever recorded, and provides quite a contrast to the rest of the album.

9. 'Ships in the Night'

Probably the album's strangest track, and the longest at five minutes, the first minute or so of this consists of eerie lost-in-space sound effects followed by a few seconds of drum beats before the first verse. There is a definite Far Eastern, oriental flavour to the music and keyboard work, plus a brief spot of lead guitar soloing in similar vein, with interesting lyrics about travelling, and a plea to 'carry me back to earth at one point'. Near the end, a slightly distorted deep voice breaks in, with an intriguing reference about the world being taken over by the Japanese.

Michael de Albuquerque

We May Be Cattle But We've All Got Names

UK: Released 1973, RCA
Currently unavailable
Personnel: Michael de Albuquerque: vocals, piano, acoustic guitar
Ollie Halsall: guitar, synthesiser, vocals
Gordon Beck: piano (tracks 1, 2, 4, 7)
John Taylor: piano (track 7)
Chris Laurence: bass guitar
Robin Sylvester: bass guitar (track 6)
Brian Bennett: drums (tracks 1, 4, 8)
Gerry Conway: drums (tracks 2, 3, 5, 6, 7)
Frank Ricotti: percussion, vibes
B. J. Cole: dobro (track 2), pedal steel guitar (track 3)
Stan Saltzman: saxophone (track 5)
Alan Skidmore: saxophone (track 8)
Chris Pine: trombone (track 5)
Henry Lowther: trumpet (track 5)
John Uckeridge: trumpet (track 5)
David Katz: strings (track 6)
Recorded at De Lane Lea Studios, Trident Studios, January–May 1973
Produced by Stuart Taylor and Michael De Albuquerque

Even before joining ELO, Michael de Albuquerque was no stranger to the recording studio. He had already released an album with percussionist Frank Ricotti (*First Wind*) in 1971, credited to Ricotti & Albuquerque—thus beyond the scope of this book. As a solo performer, his work was very different to that of the group of which he had become a member, being more in a jazz-funk groove. It is interesting to note that when Lynne was recruiting a new bass guitarist after the personnel shake-up that followed the departure of Wood, Hunt, and McDowell in the summer of 1972, the two names recommended by staff at United Artists Records were Alan Gorrie, who was about to form The Average White Band, and de Albuquerque, for the latter's solo material was in very much the same vein as AWB. He recorded this first album shortly after joining ELO.

The title, or rather the song that would give the album its title, was inspired by a comment his mother had made while she was sitting in the queue of a local surgery, when one of the nurses came out and issued people waiting with numbered tickets. As the sound of a voice on the tannoy called out his mother's number, she became quite indignant, declaring loudly: 'We may be cattle but we've all got names'.

Tracks

1. 'Dribble Dribble' (de Albuquerque)

Instrumentally this sounds very Stevie Wonder-influenced, driven along by the dual keyboards of Albuquerque and Beck. Albuquerque and Halsall trade vocal lines, sometimes breaking into scat singing and other times into falsetto. Halsall's guitar solo about halfway through is particularly fine.

2. 'Oh Woman' (de Albuquerque)

The only track on which Albuquerque plays acoustic guitar, this is a more laid-back number, with a funky backbeat but more of a blues structure. Beck's electric piano runs give it a jazzy edge towards the end.

3. 'Occasion' (de Albuquerque)

The introduction features the pedal steel guitar and lead guitar complementing each other, then the song becomes a mid-tempo soul tune, with jazzy undertones from the vibes and an almost velvet-sounding electric piano. The last seventy-five seconds take it up a gear with a blazing guitar solo into the fadeout.

4. 'We May Be Cattle But We've All Got Names' (de Albuquerque)

Albuquerque's mother may have given the record its title, but the title song does not actually feature these words in the lyrics, a song with a less than specific theme of self-discovery along the lines of 'know who you are'. Again, a mid-tempo soul-funk tune suddenly changes tack shortly before the end with a forceful guitar and synthesiser break and the vocals become more dramatic, almost screaming at points.

5. 'Do Right' (de Albuquerque)

Released as a single, the lyrical theme, like that of the previous track, is more or less one of self-awareness, in the best singer-songwriter tradition of making the listener think and not make the subject matter too obvious. Musically, it is one of the smoother soul-funk tracks on the record to start with, being introduced by warm electric piano notes and given added colour with the brass section. About a minute before the end, it takes flight and adds a storming saxophone.

6. 'My Darling Girl' (de Albuquerque)

This is the gentlest and most unashamedly romantic song on the album, and its creator's favourite; while not quite a ballad, it comes pretty close, with vocals crooned in relaxed style. It features prominent use of strings (how could a member of ELO record a solo album without strings somewhere) and saxophone, and again, there is a subtle shift in tempo towards the end, where the vocals become more impassioned just before the fade. It was later recorded by Tim Hardin on *Nine*, the last album he completed before his death in 1980.

7. 'Sweet Mirth' (de Albuquerque)

Like the preceding song, this is a smooth soul ballad, and it would take little imagination to imagine someone such as Marvin Gaye, one of the singer's heroes, covering this. Albuquerque's vocal frequently breaks into falsetto, to a backing of restrained drums and bass, with velvet-sounding pianos at first, until a startling yet controlled scream paves the way for some jazzy guitar from Halsall in the break.

8. 'Catharsis' (de Albuquerque)

After a relaxed saxophone intro, this slips into a more up-tempo jazz-funk groove, once again with a good deal of falsetto vocal, with more guitar on the break and saxes.

Stalking the Sleeper

UK: Released 1976, Warner Bros
Currently unavailable
Personnel: Michael de Albuquerque: vocals, guitars, bass guitar
Ollie Halsall: guitar (tracks 3,5)
Mike Moran: keyboards
Frank Ricotti: percussion, vibes, string and brass arrangements, saxophone (track 1)
Stan Saltzman: saxophone (track 2)
Barry Morgan: drums
Recorded at Morgan Studios, January–March 1976
Produced by Michael and George De Albuquerque

About a year after leaving ELO for family reasons, de Albuquerque visited the London headquarters of Warner Brothers to see Derek Taylor, the former press officer for The

Beatles and now a senior executive with the record company, to discuss plans with him for recording a second solo album. 'To my disbelief, and it seems more unbelievable in the present day, he saw me, right there and then,' he said nearly thirty years later. Co-produced by de Albuquerque and his brother, this had its roots in jazz and soul like the first solo venture, although with more use of strings this time round, a little closer to blue-eyed soul tinged with British prog-rock, and not surprisingly the odd little nod to the group from which he had amicably departed. No singles were released, ironically perhaps as soul music had caught on in a big way in Britain during the previous eighteen months or so; with the right promotion, this album could have enjoyed some chart success.

Tracks

1. 'I Gotta Woman' (Ray Charles)

This is the only cover version on either of these albums; it was recorded by Ray Charles in 1954 and many others since then, including The Beatles on a BBC session in 1963 under the title 'I Got a Woman'. These earlier readings were more in a rock 'n' roll tradition, in the style generally associated with Bo Diddley, though de Albuquerque brought more of a Philly soul sound with a funkier beat and strings. A vocal that veers between the gravelly sound of its writer and a Barry Gibb falsetto sits comfortably with the arrangement, which includes a short break with nothing but percussion and a saxophone solo.

2. 'Stalking the Sleeper' (Michael de Albuquerque)

From a brooding introduction with piano and strings, this mid-tempo song builds up to a huge-sounding chorus, similar to the sound Supertramp were starting to make their own. Saxophone and lead guitar take over before it fades out.

3. 'Patience Cousin!' (Michael de Albuquerque)

Michael's favourite track on the album is entirely instrumental apart from a few snatches of dialogue that have no connection with the title about halfway through— culminating in Ricotti assuring us that 'the cheque's in the post'. A voice box guitar introduction is followed by vibes on a mid-tempo funk workout, again reminiscent of the Average White Band.

4. 'The Wreckers' (Michael de Albuquerque)

A slow, almost relaxed, jazzy groove with piano, strings, and fretless bass behind the vocals, somewhat Peter Gabriel-like, on the verse pave the way for another dramatic chorus. Strings and lead guitar add extra colour towards the end.

5. 'Say What You Want' (Michael de Albuquerque)

Probably the funkiest track of all, the vocals are at their grittiest on this, with an up-tempo song in the Isley Brothers groove. Sturdy bass and drums and a dazzling guitar break are topped off to perfection by the smoking horn section.

6. 'Just Your Love' (Michael de Albuquerque)

Sprightly strings and mid-tempo blue-eyed soul, underpinned by the brass section, and 'who-hoo' backing vocals, edge this one nearer the pop-soul market. There is a nod to the sound that the Four Seasons, on a high with their 'December 1963 (Oh What a Night)', had adopted around this time, and an engaging saxophone break.

7. 'Walking out on Sunny Street' (Michael de Albuquerque)

A song that floats between romance and good-time feeling starts off slowly with lush strings before building up towards an instantly commercial chorus—a frequently used but effective device on this album.

8. 'Tonight on the Highway' (Michael de Albuquerque)

Again, a quiet introduction, with harp and soft strings, gather pace into another song that call Peter Gabriel, Genesis, and Supertramp to mind, leading to a crescendo of lead guitar, saxophone, and an explosion courtesy of the string section.

Kelly Groucutt

Kelly

UK: Released 1982, RCA
US: Released 1983, Riva
Currently unavailable
Personnel: Kelly Groucutt: vocals, bass guitar, guitars, keyboards
Bev Bevan: drums
Richard Tandy: keyboards
Mik Kaminski: violin
Louis Clark: string arrangements
Recorded 1981 at 54 East Sound Recorders, Pasadena, CA; The Old Smithy Studios, Worcester
Produced by Kelly Groucutt

Groucutt joined ELO in 1974, replacing de Albuquerque as bass guitarist and backing vocalist during the recording of *Eldorado*. He began writing songs soon afterwards, initially just for fun, but more seriously around the time that *Out of the Blue* was being recorded. Unlike the musician whom he replaced, his songs sounded much more like those of the group. *Kelly* was more or less an ELO album without Lynne, recorded while the others had time to spare in 1981, with Groucutt's songs and lead vocal. Like George Harrison, Dave Davies, and John Entwistle, Groucutt was overshadowed by a more prolific and proven partnership or writer (although the other three generally managed one or two songs on most Beatles, Kinks, and Who albums), and he had to look for solo albums for artistic fulfilment. 'I was looking for an outlet of my own,' he said shortly after release, 'Jeff obviously doesn't need any help with the writing, so this seemed a natural step.' Most fans agree that he was an excellent singer, although not in the same league as Lynne as a songwriter. Neither album nor the two singles received any significant promotion or airplay, and they failed to chart. The album was 'digitally tweaked' in 2001 and a limited edition for fans, with two bonus tracks, was issued on his own label Li'l Jenny Records in 2001.

When it was suggested to Groucutt that it sounded similar to ELO in performance and arrangement, he said that the music the group played was his kind of music, and that was therefore what he had put on his own album: 'Most group members who do solo albums usually have a totally different sound, but I love ELO's music, and I write that way'. Overall, it has generally been compared unfavourably with the group's later albums and arguably suffers from unambitious production, Kelly's own, suggesting it might have benefited from a more experienced outside co-producer to exploit the songs and ideas better. Even so, any objective fan prepared to acknowledge that Lynne did not have a monopoly of talent as a writer will find it well worth seeking out.

Groucutt reworked 'Am I a Dreamer', backed with 'I'll Cry For You Tonight', on a single released under the alias Player (not to be confused with the American group of that name who had a late 1970s hit with 'Baby Come Back') on the Rainbow label, but with no more success the second time round.

Two songs, 'Dear Mama' and 'Sea of Dreams', also appeared on *Beyond the Dream* by OrKestra, a group featuring Groucutt, Kaminski, and McDowell, released in 1993. They are probably rerecordings, although they sound very close to the originals.

Tracks

1. 'Am I a Dreamer' (Kelly Groucutt)

The first single has the benefit of gloriously cascading, extravagant strings and keyboards, to say nothing of an instant hook. Like several of the other tracks, it would not have sounded out of place on one of the last couple of ELO albums.

2. 'Oh, Little Darling' (Kelly Groucutt)

The second single sounds a little dated, although that is not intended as criticism. The tempo shows similarities with early work by The Beach Boys and The Four Seasons, with a touch of pizzicato string effects reminiscent of Buddy Holly's more easy listening output, and colourful harmony vocals further on in the song.

3. 'Dear Mama' (Kelly Groucutt)

A ballad with piano and strings, this is about a young soldier writing home to his mother, convinced that this will be his last letter home before he is killed in the war, and he gives a genuinely emotional vocal performance.

4. 'Black-Hearted Woman' (Kelly Groucutt)

This is the most out-and-out dance-orientated track, with a nod to 'Last Train to London' in its funky guitar, keyboards, and bass, and with lyrics about a femme fatale.

5. 'Midnight Train' (Kelly Groucutt)

This starts off with train sound effects, then breaks into a snappy hoedown country song about 'getting out of town' to discover a new life. Kaminski's unmistakable fiddle adds a touch of colour. Groucutt was keen on country music, and in an interview shortly before the demise of ELO Part II, he suggested that in future he might become involved in that particular scene.

6. 'Can't Stand the Morning' (Kelly Groucutt)

One of the strongest tunes. Underpinned by piano and guitar, prominent strings, and an insistent hook in the chorus, this would have been a strong contender for a single, had either of the first two tracks fared better.

7. 'Anything Goes With Me' (Kelly Groucutt)

The album's second ballad is couched mainly in strings and acoustic guitar. A George Harrison-flavoured guitar solo makes a welcome appearance during the break.

8. 'Old Rock 'n' Roller' (Kelly Groucutt)

The album's fun track, on which a fuzzy electric rhythm guitar and sprightly piano underpin the verses, with a lead guitar solo and one or two asides from an uncredited female vocalist, evoking the call-and-respond lines in 'Summertime Blues'.

9. 'Don't Wanna Hear That Song' (Kelly Groucutt)

A pleasant mid-tempo number, in the vein of the others although not so strong.

10. 'You've Been Telling Lies' (Kelly Groucutt)

This begins slowly with piano and strings and Beatle-like backing vocals. After the first couple of verses, it takes on an almost reggae rhythm, followed by a synthesiser break.

11. 'You Don't Need to Hold Me Tight' (Kelly Groucutt)

Another mid-tempo song with more cascading strings, and good use of falsetto vocals.

12. 'Sea of Dreams' (Kelly Groucutt)

This is by far the most ambitious track here, as well as the longest at five minutes, suggesting an attempt to emulate some of ELO's epics from the 1970s. Crashing waves and a few bars from a string quartet, as opposed to the usual rush of strings, are followed by acoustic guitar leading to the first verse. The string quartet theme at the start is repeated after a couple of minutes, first of all on a keyboard sounding like harpsichords, then repeated with strings in different keys, acting as a bridge to the second and much slower part of the song, with vocals through a vocoder at first, then the repeated phrase 'I'm coming home', which fades out into a finale of further wave sound effects to a peaceful conclusion.

2001 Bonus Tracks

13. 'I'll Cry for You Tonight' (Kelly Groucutt)

This is perhaps the least successful track of all. A rather mawkish ballad with strings, it is not helped by lyrics of the 'I'll squeeze my pillow and hold you tight' variety.

14. 'Am I a Dreamer' (Kelly Groucutt)

A remix of the first track, with Kaminski's violin playing a more prominent role.

Louis Clark

'(per-spek-tiv) n'

UK: Released March 1979, Jet
US Unreleased

Current edition: Edsel CD
Personnel: Louis Clark: keyboards, guitars, bass guitar, flutes, recorders
Graham Todd: keyboards
Francis Monkman: keyboards
John Tout: keyboards
Paul Robbins: keyboards
Hartley Cain: guitar
Ricky Hitchcock: guitar
Keith Jenkins: guitar
Dick Plant: guitar
Kevin Peek: guitar synthesiser
Roy Wood: guitar sitar
Simon Phillips: drums
Peter Van Hooke: drums
Nick Pentelow: saxophone
George Henry: orchestral contractor
Recorded at Music Centre Studios, Wembley; DJM Studios, London, 1978
Produced by Louis Clark

Clark made several albums with the Royal Philharmonic Orchestra, most famously *Hooked On Classics* at the time of the medley craze in 1981 in the wake of Starsound's 'Stars on 45' and several imitators who released medleys from their back catalogue as singles. Three years earlier, he had recorded what was, in effect, his only solo LP. Musically, it is akin to several of Mike Oldfield's albums in the tradition of *Tubular Bells*, consisting of one piece of instrumental music on each side of the album (on vinyl) or two separate pieces (on CD), both lasting around twenty-three minutes each and incorporating several distinct movements that are each given their own title. A glance at the credits reveals a total absence of ELO members among the other musicians, as they were taking part in the *Out of the Blue* world tour when it was recorded. The personnel include Roy Wood; former Wizzard member Nick Pentelow; former Wizzo Band member Paul Robbins; John Tout of Renaissance; plus Francis Monkman and Kevin Peek, two of the musicians who were then in the process of helping to form Sky.

Tracks

1. 'Escape/Interlude 1 (Reminiscence)/Andante (The Long Trek)/Interlude 2 (Nostalgia)/ Allegro Vivo (On the Run)/Lento (Departure)'

Any record of this nature is bound to be compared to the works of Mike Oldfield, and perhaps suffer as a result. However, Clark's *magnum opus* as composer, arranger, conductor, and producer can certainly hold its own against the more famous album that led the way. Side one begins with a sound like thunder gradually increasing in volume, followed by an explosion and a delightfully bombastic interlude on church organ, reminiscent of George

Martin's 'Theme One'. Next comes an energetic bustling theme in which strings and drums form the backdrop to a theme led by guitar sitar. After about four minutes, it comes almost to a halt, the effect being similar to that of the 'Overture' to *Eldorado* or the light and shade in the Gilbert and Sullivan Savoy Operas overtures, with slow and fast movements alternating—and fuses into a gentler passage dominated by whistling synthesiser and crisp chords on an acoustic guitar. Thereafter, the piece is one of shifting rhythms, tempos, and textures. A funeral march-like tune flows seamlessly into about ninety seconds-worth of a semi-bluesy section led by electric guitar, strings, drums and the occasional popping of syn-drums—something that almost every record of the era featured somewhere. Dream-like passages yield to more energetic moments, such as the one about halfway through where a rock 'n' roll-inspired section manages to combine playful, cascading strings that call to mind the orchestral passages in John Miles's 'Music', a burst that sounds as if it was inspired by Ron Goodwin's '633 Squadron' theme—Little Richard-style piano, touches of the choir that sang on part of 'Out of the Blue', a movement played first on lead guitar and then repeated by the strings, and saxophone. For the last five minutes or so, it slows down and the strings take full rein with an air that might be likened to a funeral march.

'Escape' and 'Departure', the opening and closing sections, were issued on both sides of a single about four months after the album.

2. 'Winter Quotation/Conflictions/Interlude 3 (Euphoria)/The Test/Fulfilment/Into the Mysterious/Canzonet/Fugue/Dance of Joy/Finale'

Side two opens with a few bars of sawing violins and electric guitar, joined within a minute or so by drums and then jangling guitars, until one almost expects The Byrds to start singing. It is the preface to a passage that is almost rock 'n' roll in its construction, similar to the effect of 'Illusions in G Major' or 'Rockaria!', with a tune starting like a twelve-bar blues and, shortly before the end of the verse, adding two additional chords, which takes it in a different direction entirely. The tune is then taken up by lead guitar and strings, then, as it slows down briefly, a choir starts to sing and saxophone returns. About six minutes in, it yields to a softer orchestral theme for about a minute, then returns to the rock 'n' roll theme with what is surely the most ELO-like part in either piece on the record. Some momentary dips in tempo follow, with a breathtaking amount of light and shade or bombast and tranquillity. A few seconds of classical guitar with strings in the background make their appearance at one point. At length, the strings play a sprightly, playful classical-style theme, with rapid moments close to a Scherzo in a Beethoven Symphony. About four minutes are dominated by an Irish jig, led by synthesiser and acoustic guitar, with fiddle and then full orchestra joining in. A short choral interlude punctuates it before the jig resumes, faster than before and coming to an almost breathless end. The last three minutes comprise a grand finale, rising to a crescendo of almost Wagnerian proportions with strings and choir, a stately conclusion—and another short explosion at the end.

As with Part One, it is tempting to namecheck other pieces of music to which moments bear some likeness. One can suggest some of the wordless vocals on Focus's 'Hocus Pocus', the stirring movements on Elton John's 'Funeral for a Friend', or epic passages from Jeff Wayne's *War of the Worlds*—one of the biggest-selling albums in Britain around the time this was recorded. By the end, the listener is left with a sense of having been on a complete musical journey of sorts.

Endnotes

Chapter 1

1. *The Guardian*, 30 March 2016
2. Bevan, B., *The The Electric Light Orchestra Story*, p.42
3. www.thequietus.com, 2 November 2015
4. *New Musical Express*, 11 April 1976
5. *Face the Music* fanzine (13), 1992
6. *Sounds*, 20 September 1974
7. *Circus*, 17 January 1977
8. *The Guardian*, 30 March 2016
9. ELOfans News, elofans.com, 4 February 2015
10. Jeff Lynne, on *Zoom*, www.ftmusic.com/discography/elo/zoom/, 2001
11. Jeff Lynne, Electric Light Orchestra—Up Close US Jones Radio Network Radio Show, jefflynnesongs.com, July 2001

Chapter 2

1. *Face the Music* fanzine (9), 1991

Chapter 3

1. *The Guardian*, 20 November 2015
2. *The Sun*, www.songfacts.com, 2015
3. *Paste Magazine* online, pastemagazine.com, 10 November 2015

Chapter 4

1 *Billboard*, www.billboard.com, 26 September 2012

Chapter 5

1. *Face the Music* fanzine (7), 1990
2. Ultimate Classic Rock, ultimateclassicrock.com/jeff-lynne-solo-album/, 1 August 2012
3. Jeff Lynne Song Database, www.jefflynnesongs.com/jlworks1.php
4. Jeb Wright: Jeff Lynne, a blast from the past, www.classicrockrevisited.com, 2012
5. Only Solitaire, starling.rinet.ru/music/roywood.htm
6. *Keep On Rockin* fanzine (3), 1992

All websites accessed August–November 2016

Bibliography

Books

Arden, D., and Wall, M., *Mr Big: Ozzy, Sharon and my life as the Godfather of Rock* (London: Robson, 2004)
Bevan, B., *The Electric Light Orchestra Story* (London: Mushroom, 1980)
Frame, P., *The Complete Rock Family Trees* (London: Omnibus, 1983)
Guttenbacher, P., Haines, M., & von Petersdorff, A., *Unexpected Messages: The Story of the Electric Light Orchestra, The Move, Jeff Lynne, Roy Wood, Bev Bevan, including all members and related artists' projects with the complete world discography* (Villingen, Germany: FTM Germany, 1996)
Scott-Morgan, D., *Patterns in the Chaos: Reflections in Sawdust* (Birmingham: Lifeware, 2014)
Van der Kiste, J., *Jeff Lynne: The Electric Light Orchestra: Before and After* (Stroud: Fonthill, 2015); *Roy Wood: The Move, Wizzard, and Beyond* (South Brent: A&F/CreateSpace, 2014)
Wanda, J., *Blackberry Way: Move, Electric Light Orchestra, Roy Wood, Jeff Lynne und Steve Gibbons Band* (Balve, Germany: Star Cluster, 1996)

Websites

Cherry Blossom Clinic: www.cherryblossomclinic.freeserve.co.uk/
ELO and Jeff Lynne: www.elo.biz/
ELOBF (Beatles Forever): elobeatlesforever.blogspot.com/
Face the Music online: www.ftmusic.com/
Jeff Lynne & Electric Light Orchestra, Discovery: www.elodiscovery.com/
Jeff Lynne Song Database: www.jefflynnesongs.com/
Showdown, Jeff Lynne mailing list: www.eskimo.com/~noanswer/move_archives/movearchives.html
45cat, vinyl database: www.45cat.com/
Discogs, vinyl and CD database: www.discogs.com/